Mike Faverman and Pat Mac

ULTIMATE CAMP COOKING

Andrews McMeel
Publishing, LLC
Kansas City · Sydney · London

11 12 13 14 15 WKT 10 9 8 7 6 5 4 3 2 1

ISBN: 978-1-4494-0159-7

Library of Congress Control Number:
2010930549

www.ultimatecampcooking.com

www.andrewsmcmeel.com

I dedicate this book to my parents, Howard and Diane Faverman. They were such terrible cooks it pushed me to experiment with food. I couldn't be any worse than them! I learned quickly to experiment and take risks, and then serendipitously became great. This is what ultimately makes a person a master chef. Keep being inquisitive with your food and one day you will be a master of flavor.

I also dedicate this to my extremely talented and intelligent Aunt Sheila. She passed away recently from her battle with cancer. It would've been my dream to work on this cookbook together with her. She was a huge inspiration and influence on my career, and I will miss her brilliance for the rest of my life. Rest in peace.

—Mike Faverman

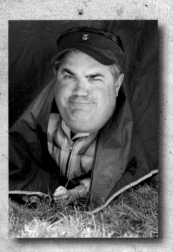

I dedicate this book to my father, Michael McAllister, who owned his own bar and restaurant. He was smart enough to sell it before I was old enough to take it over. He put me to work in the kitchen at a young enough age to learn culinary skills and taught me to be creative with recipes.

I also dedicate this to my wife's parents, Grant and Norma Gillette, for initiating me into the world of camping by purchasing camping and cooking equipment for me. They knew what they were doing by jump-starting my culinary craft by giving me the tools to create.

Finally, I would like to dedicate this book to my brother-in-law, Dexter McBride, for planting the seed to combine my love of comedy, cooking, and camping into a career.

—Pat Mac

Contents

About Ultimate Camp Cooking

by Mike Faverman

The Beginning

Pat and I met at an open mike night at the Laff Stop on West Gray in Houston, Texas, in 2001. We were both touring as stand-up comedians and ended up on a Monday night at one of the most popular open mikes in the country at the time. I watched Pat and could tell he was a seasoned pro. He also must've seen me as he was raving about how much better I was than he at the time. (At least that's how I saw it.) We kept in touch over the next few years, e-mailing and on the rare occasion speaking on the phone. Pat is one of the nicest people I've ever met, which is one of the things that make me most annoyed about him. I'm a bit of a negative, caustic, and abrasive personality and he's the guy who laughs hysterically at everyone's jokes. He really takes life in and I vehemently spit life out, after chewing it up quite a bit.

Pat lived in Boise, Idaho, for all of his life. I was always trying to get work at the Funny Bone Comedy Club there. It was known as one of the country's best-kept secrets. The city

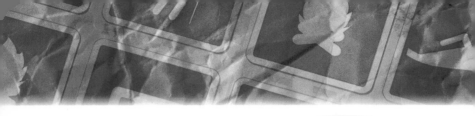

had a female-to-male ratio of nine women to one man. There were a lot of cute women in that city. At that time, I was single and looking for some fun. I had been rejected several times by the comedy club's owner, then Pat and my buddy Brian took over the booking of the club. This was my chance to work at the club and see my friend again in the cool city of Boise.

I flew up to Boise from L.A. Brian, who is like the unofficial governor of Boise, picked me up. We got to the club and walked across the street to a corporate show that Pat was working at Boise State University. I watched Pat on stage and remembered the guy he was and the style of comedy he performed. Pat is a very fun loving and relatable comedian. He speaks about topics such as marriage, eating, and the frustrations of life, but in a light and fun way. On the other hand, I speak about stupid people and sex, and I make fun of everything in an abrasive and caustic manner. We were polar opposites in demeanor and style.

As the week went on, the crowds really enjoyed the shows

and my style of comedy. It's a drinking and partying city that loves its women fast and its comedy dirty. At the end of the week, the staff decided to throw a barbecue for me. After the barbecue started no one was in the kitchen cooking and serving food except for Pat and me. We were dominating the grill and serving different meals to all the drunken employees. Pat mentioned that the place everyone loves to congregate at a party was the kitchen. I agreed and we started talking about our love of food and passion for cooking.

talked about being a chef at several restaurants around the country and Pat told me stories about how his dad owned and operated a restaurant in the years past and how he worked for $2.00 an hour when he was a child. He also mentioned how he too loved the fast pace and the personal relationships his family had with the clientele. He loved food and admired the people who could put such a delicious plate together in a short amount of time and make it seem effortless. Pat also told me how he used to go in the woods and build this enormous kitchen with all the equipment he'd accumulated over the past ten years. He said it was amazing how fast people would wander over to his site and ask questions about the different surfaces and the different meals he'd been preparing. He told me that random people

would visit his site and before he knew it, they would be exchanging phone numbers, e-mails, and contact info as they became friends through food and laughter. This was my passion as well. We had thought we were polar opposites, but it turned out we had more in common than we thought.

The Making of Our First DVD

y favorite two things in the world happen to be making people laugh and making meals people enjoy. Pat and I joked about making a cooking DVD that incorporated comedy and cooking. As we laughed, it came to my mind that this wouldn't be too difficult.

I had directed some short films, documentaries, and commercials. Maybe I could bring a small crew in the woods, make a DVD, edit it, and duplicate it for people to see. It would be cheap. We scheduled a time for me to travel to Boise to work the club and break away for a few days to film our DVD.

For two people who have never worked together before, we were pretty organized and attentive to details. There was no arguing and it began to seem to us that this dream could actually turn into a reality. We loaded up Pat's pop-up tent trailer with a list of recipes, a bunch of groceries, and some blank DVDs, and headed for the mountains in McCall, Idaho. We set up camp at Ponderosa State Park in September. Because Pat had done

this many times in the past, the setup was fast and efficient. I taped it to show people how easy and fast you can get situated in the woods. I guess our initial purpose was to encourage people not only to cook while in the outdoors, but to get away from all the technology and stress of life and bring their conscious mind into the calm and serene woods where the only thing you can hear is nature and the voices of others who are enjoying the outdoors as well.

At first it was a bit too quiet for me. I've always lived in the city and I find the sounds of traffic and people congregating in the streets kind of cozy. It was going to be difficult to share bed space with crickets and other loud, annoying insects that seemed to be mocking the

city boy in the woods. However, I couldn't believe how quickly I warmed up to the quiet and the calmness of the people around us. Everyone seemed relaxed and peaceful, which is rare in the city. You say hello to some-one in the streets of a big city and they think you are mentally ill. ("Did he just say hello to me? What a freak!")

Everyone seemed interested in us and what we had planned for the evening. To be completely honest, when people first laid eyes on both Pat and me with our video camera out, they thought we were a couple. They cracked jokes about Brokeback camping!!! I got mad, because if you saw what I looked like, you'd think I could do a lot better than Pat! We squashed that rumor really fast as we comically approached the people who spread the rumor and asked them to our first dinner.

Pat told me that if we built a kitchen, they would come. I didn't think that was the way it worked. People are pretty private when it comes to sharing space and butt-ing into other people's business, or so I thought. However, when people are in the outdoors all the rules seem to change. As soon as

our kitchen was complete and the flames hit the grill, and the aroma of marinated meats and sautéed vegetables hit the air, it was as if an imaginary dinner bell was rung. People started coming out of the

woodwork—or the woods, in this case. They started asking ques-tions, such as, "Where did you get that grill?" "What are you cook-ing?" and "Who are you guys?"

We explained to everyone that we were filming a camp cooking DVD and we wanted people to be a part of it. We had free food and all they needed to do was come over when all the food was done. "Sounds easy enough," they said, so Pat and I got to work filming and preparing our recipes.

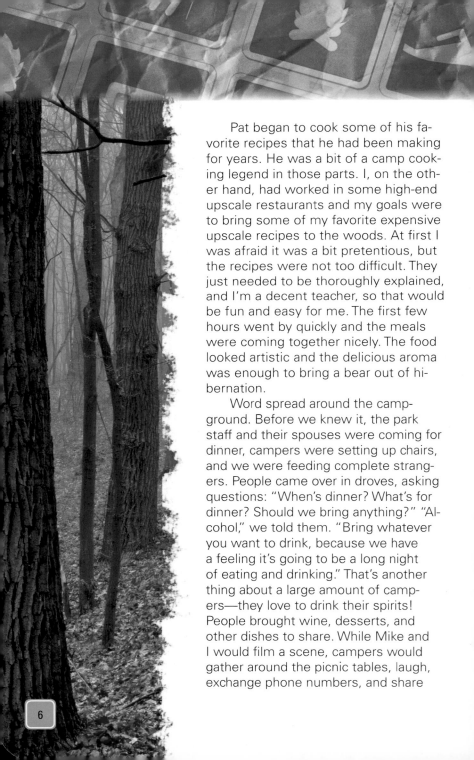

Pat began to cook some of his favorite recipes that he had been making for years. He was a bit of a camp cooking legend in those parts. I, on the other hand, had worked in some high-end upscale restaurants and my goals were to bring some of my favorite expensive upscale recipes to the woods. At first I was afraid it was a bit pretentious, but the recipes were not too difficult. They just needed to be thoroughly explained, and I'm a decent teacher, so that would be fun and easy for me. The first few hours went by quickly and the meals were coming together nicely. The food looked artistic and the delicious aroma was enough to bring a bear out of hibernation.

Word spread around the campground. Before we knew it, the park staff and their spouses were coming for dinner, campers were setting up chairs, and we were feeding complete strangers. People came over in droves, asking questions: "When's dinner? What's for dinner? Should we bring anything?" "Alcohol," we told them. "Bring whatever you want to drink, because we have a feeling it's going to be a long night of eating and drinking." That's another thing about a large amount of campers—they love to drink their spirits! People brought wine, desserts, and other dishes to share. While Mike and I would film a scene, campers would gather around the picnic tables, laugh, exchange phone numbers, and share

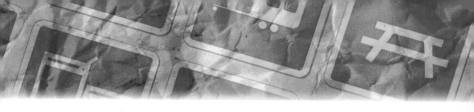

the whiskey that some campers had brought to the table. People came over to sample each recipe and I couldn't believe the excitement, though, truth be told, I'm not sure if it was the free food or the flavor. Pat and I quickly realized that this was going to work and work well. We watched our idea transcend cooking and comedy, bringing people together to make new friends and have good times that they would remember for the rest of their lives. And at the time we had no idea how many people would later touch our lives through food, fun, and laughter.

Pat and I sat down that night in front of a nice healthy fire talking about the success of our day and the potential of what we created. We needed a catchy name. Ultimate Camp Cooking? I liked it, but it didn't incorporate the comedy aspect of our DVD series. We decided the comedy was a bonus, and it wasn't necessary for it to be in the name, so we stuck with it and called ourselves comedian chefs. I'm glad we did, as the name stands for great cooking in the outdoors and the laughter that comes along with it. That's what we were really

all about in the first place.

As days passed, dozens of people visited our campsite, were fed, and left with new friends and full stomachs. Pat and I had stumbled on a hit and it was time to parlay its potential into something big. I went home and started editing the footage. It was such a beautiful shoot, combining the beauty of nature and the beauty of food. Sprinkled in was the beauty of people having fun and laughing. This was a project of positive vibes and good energy, and it was going to be something that would grow in success over a short amount of time, because everyone likes to eat and laugh.

I finished editing the DVD and watched it several times to make sure it was what I wanted to show the world. I couldn't believe how real it was, with nothing rehearsed and everything off the cuff. What had started as a project that we had no idea what we were trying to capture quickly sculpted itself into a clear vision as if we had planned it all along. We had created a reality movie about cooking and bringing people together through laughter and food. It quickly became a huge hit.

The Birth of Our Live Performances

As manager of the Funny Bone Comedy Club in Boise, Pat thought that maybe if we threw a DVD release party we would be able to gauge the interest of people with a passion for outdoor cooking. We decided to put on a little show onstage with all the people who had participated in the filming of the DVD. It was a great turnout. TV people covered it, several radio stations interviewed us, and hundreds of people showed up to see the premiere. They were laughing and eating the food Pat and I prepared for the show.

After the show ended, people lined up all the way out the doors to buy the DVD. We sold over a thousand dollars' worth of DVDs in a matter of

thirty minutes after our show. What was happening here? When I got back to Los Angeles I immediately researched camping, RVs, and the outdoor lifestyle and found millions of groups, clubs, and organizations that supported lovers of the outdoors. I even stumbled on a few companies that have RV and camping shows at convention centers to help distribute fifth wheels, toy haulers, RVs, ATVs, and such. Best of all, they hire entertainment for these events.

We got in touch with a guy named Kevin Renfro who was in charge of the entire Indianapolis Boat, Sport, and Travel Show. He listened to us pitch what an awesome show we had and what a great job we would do if we got hired to entertain at his show. Somehow he agreed and the next thing we knew we were hired to entertain at

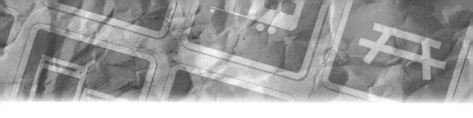

his huge ten-day RV event. We were freaking out because we didn't have a live show and we were being paid a lot of money to get the job done. After several weeks of deliberations we came up with what we thought would be a fun and interesting show. The only problem is we had no way to practice. Since Pat and I live in different cities and never get to see each other, there was no other choice but to do it for the first time at the event.

The event was huge! There was something like 250,000 square feet of space, thousands of RVs, trailers, ATVs, boats, and the like. It was very intimidating. We spent the first day putting up our set, which consisted of a wooden bear we borrowed from an exhibitor, an ATV borrowed from a vendor, and an RV from one of the dealers. The set looked great—like we were camping with an

outdoor kitchen, outdoor grill, a Dutch oven, and props. All we needed was a show. I had written out a manuscript and we felt confident that if we kept to the format we would get by and even learn along the way. I was partially right. Turns out these shows are not ideal for stand-up comedy. There's too much light, high ceilings, and too many distractions to keep people from paying attention to the show, so we had to learn to play with the elements a bit. In order to make the people watch and listen we needed to be more interactive with our audiences—ask questions, give people a hard time, involve them in the act. As the week progressed it all started to come together. The jokes lined up, the interaction became natural, and we created catch-phrases. Pat and I sold over 800 DVDs in that ten-day period. We were ecstatic!

Onward to RV and Trade Shows

course that was a bit of an exaggeration, but we thought our show was cool, and after some begging and pleading, he decided to give us the chance to work at his Pomona show. It was one of his smaller events and needed good entertainment. It could lead to many more events for us.

We showed up at the event and not knowing what Tom looked like, we saw a guy walking toward us. He was not out of shape, but certainly not an athlete. He had a bit of a glow and seemed very happy with life in general. He was amiable and warm, shouting, "Here are the stars!" I liked him right off the bat. He showed us where we were going to perform, and we thanked him and took a tour of the grounds. We set up our grills and figured out what would be best for our show. There was a bit of a problem: We usually perform inside convention centers and this show was entirely outside in the scalding sun with the wind blowing all our cups and napkins everywhere.

When we returned from our first trade show we wanted more. I began to research camping and RV shows, and I found a company named Affinity. This company had dozens of publications, membership groups, directories, and most importantly an event division that had approximately forty events a year. That could keep us busy for years!

We put a call into the events division, eventually getting in touch with Tom Gaither, the senior vice president of events. He was a great guy, but he seemed a little skeptical at first, probably because so many people call and pitch their ideas to him. We told him we had a hot comedy cooking show and had done events for years. Of

The first day of the event arrived and we were ready to go as the crowds of people strolled around the grounds looking for ridiculous deals on amazing RVs. The first show was dismal. Our performance was pretty good, but there were only a few people. Pat and I had vast experience of touring as a stand-up comedians. It was tough dealing with people who didn't know exactly what we were bringing to the table. The second show was a lot better as the word got out. The show also got tighter. The fact that Pat and I have great chemistry to begin with was testament to a bright future in this business. The next day we were rolling with the shows, playing off the crowd and going with whatever was thrown our way. People began to recognize us from previous performances. Then Tom came over and told us he would be attending our next show. "Oh, no," we thought. "What if we have one of our bad shows and he fires us on the spot?" I was a bit nervous about bombing in front of the guy who put his neck on the line for us.

The show began and there was a malfunction right away. The propane ran out on one of our grills, but we quickly rectified the situation, making a joke, and quickly moved on. I watched Tom in the back of the audience. The audience was big, and I could tell they were skeptical. Pat and I moved into our fast-paced, high-energy insult act, making fun of the people in Pomona and the cities we had visited as comedians in the past. The crowd warmed up fast. Tom was looking around for the reaction of the audience. I could tell right away that he was a smart man who knew what he wanted out of his entertainment for the show. As the show moved on, I began to notice how much people loved it. We were having a great time doing what we were doing, laughing and being very playful, even when we made a few obvious mistakes. At one point, Pat and I were making fun of people from the Midwest and Tom yelled, "My wife's from Indiana!" We yelled back, "That would explain why she married you!" It got a big laugh. Tom yelled out for two reasons, first because he was caught up in the excitement and also because he wanted to see how we handled hecklers. We must have passed, because he leaned back in his chair and took in the rest of the show. I knew at that moment we had a future at his shows.

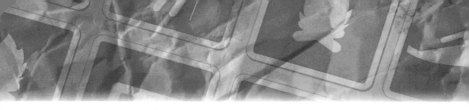

Building a Fan Base

With each event, Pat and I became stronger as performers, the show jelled, and the evolution of our creation became clearer. We had never worked so hard and had so much fun doing it. It's refreshing to make something that not only becomes successful, but also has so much potential for fun. Some shows were like pulling teeth, when people stared at us blankly as if we were a science project, but for every one of those there would be ten more where we would be swarmed with people loving our show and wanting to be part of what we were doing.

As time passed, it was strange to find that not only did we have fans, but people who followed us. They would come up to us before shows and tell us they saw us the previous year, or watch our DVD all the time and go to our Web site to watch our videos. People told us they came specifically to the show to see us again. They wanted to know if we had a new DVD or a cookbook to sell. They wanted to know what city we would be in the next and if they could come to another show later that day. One family took a train from Greensboro, North Carolina, all the way to Charlotte to see our show again because they loved the jokes and the food!

After a few more very successful events I met with Tom Gaither to explain how we could be a huge asset to his company. I told him we should have cooking jackets with the logos of his companies so that when we performed in front of huge audiences the logos would be an introduction to his companies. He liked that idea but wondered what companies would sponsor us on the road. He gave me all of the information about the companies under the Affinity umbrella, and explained to me about what each did and how we could be a part of their promotions. I went home from that meeting with a lot of information and a lot to think about. How would I convince this company to put us on the road, doing our show and promoting their companies?

The Progression

What I found out was that each company promoted fun and family in the outdoors as you camp and/or RV. That's easy enough. Who doesn't like to enjoy the great outdoors with friends and family in a safe and fun way? If that is what we needed to promote for these companies, it would be a breeze. In our show we could talk about each company and what they had to offer in such a way that it wouldn't seem like a pitch, but we could incorporate it into stories about both Pat's and my camping experiences. We'd just be sharing personal experiences that people could relate to when they were camping. Easy!

Tom loved the idea and selected a few companies we could approach for potential sponsorship. One of these was the Good Sam Club, which already had over a million members. They had been around for decades, but they needed something to help promote them and help them connect with a new generation of members. We wanted to help them do that so they could continue to enjoy a long-term membership.

I met with Joe Daquino, a very smart and confident man, an outside-of-the-box thinker, and president of the Good Sam Club. I explained to him my belief that Pat and I could bring in new blood for his club and help him multimarket through TV, radio, newspapers, and magazines. I showed him several videos of Pat and I doing live performances and an example of what our next DVD would look like with all of his companies' logos on the cover for consumers to see. Joe is a lover of both cooking and comedy. It was a perfect fit. He became a supporter almost immediately.

As the months moved on and the RV and camping season neared, I finally got the call from both Joe and Tom, getting the green light for a seven-city tour with three sponsors. This was very exciting. What had at first been a half-kidding, half-baked idea in a kitchen at a barbecue had become a national touring comedy cooking show with four major sponsors, the fourth being the Affinity events who ran the shows we would be performing.

The first year of shows was phenomenal. We met some amazing people who are now great friends and we had

crowd going, so we slipped into cruise control. The show was nose-diving into a new level of stink. It seemed like people were stuck in a coma, worrying about everything else in their lives. As we were performing, I gave Pat the silent message, "This show is in the crapper." Pat agreed, so we started to joke to ourselves about how much we loved our jobs and how great a show we were having with intense sarcasm. Out of the corner of my eye I saw a man who had to be over 100 years old. He had a long gray beard that looked like an old wicker broom, and in front of him was a walker that looked like it came from the same era when he was in high school. No joke, he was the oldest man I had ever seen in my life. He was walking at a snail's pace and seemed unable to lift his head. It was hanging down as far as it could physically be. As I told a joke, I saw him slam his head into the side of an RV that was parked there. It knocked him out, but he was still standing, propped up by the RV and his walker. If neither of those objects had been present he would have fallen to the ground. Understand that I'm not a malicious person, nor do

some hilarious experiences. There are too many to mention, but one stands out. We were working for a fine gentleman, Jeff Haughton, who ran several shows around the country and was one of the longest running show promoters in the business. He was a whiz and a great guy—loved his Marker's Mark, too! Jeff decided to bring his wife to see one of our shows. He really liked what we did and got a kick out of the spontaneous things we would do when we mingled with the audience. During one of our live shows in Charlotte, North Carolina, Pat and I were struggling to get the

I enjoy other people's pain, but this was one of the funniest things I've ever seen. Right before he hit his head, I said, "Sir, be careful," but it was too late. When I said that everyone turned to look and witnessed the whole thing. The barely awake, apathetic audience was suddenly in stitches. People were literally falling off their chairs. Pat was laughing so hysterically he could barely stay standing. He had to go off the set and into the RV that we were using as a backdrop, but he still had on his wireless microphone so the audience could hear his hysterics. I was trying to keep the show together but failing miserably. Do you ever laugh so much that no matter how hard you try to compose yourself it just escalates uncontrollably? That's what was happening to about forty people altogether. A few people found the whole scene appalling and left immediately. Pat and I are both professional comedians, and each have over ten years' experience. Comedians laugh at things most people find sad or unfunny because we're so used to seeing a situation from an angle that an average Joe wouldn't think of.

Jeff was in the audience with his wife. Luckily he liked us very much because we could have gotten in a lot of trouble for what happened, but I could see that he was laughing so hard tears were running down his face, while his wife was shaking her head in disgust. You could tell who had the warped sense of humor in that audience. What started

out as a dismal show turned into one of the funniest moments I have ever experienced during a live show. Pat was incapable of finishing that show and I did everything in my power to keep it together to no avail. By the end, people came up to us and told us that was the funniest thing they had ever seen in their lives. I would've hoped they would say that about our show, but we'll take it for what it's worth. I apologized to Jeff for the situation and he laughed out loud again. "That was one of the funniest things I've ever seen. Don't worry a second about it. That was classic!" Jeff said. Pat called me a few weeks later, laughing hysterically into the phone, telling me he was in the shower, thought about it again, and almost lost his balance he laughed so hard.

Some of you may be reading this and saying to yourself, "That's just mean seeing an old man hurt himself and no one helped him and laughing about it." We want you to know that the man came out of it just fine and had a good laugh at himself with us after the show. After he came to, he slowly walked over to our booth and bought our DVD. I'm not even sure he had a DVD player; I just think he was part of something so funny he had to buy whatever it was we were selling. Then he slowly walked off into RV heaven.

We are still touring and growing as a live show, and we add to our DVD series each year. We plan on expanding our enterprise in the years to come. We hope you enjoy our recipes. We also hope you'll visit our Web site at Ultimate-campcooking.com and check out the new recipes we'll be posting from month to month. Tell your friends about us and make sure to come check out our live shows if you haven't already. You never know what could happen—we never do!

Keep on cook'n!!!

Mike and Pat

ULTIMATE CAMP COOKING

Basics

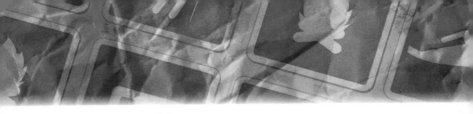

How to Plan Your Food

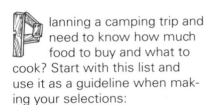

lanning a camping trip and need to know how much food to buy and what to cook? Start with this list and use it as a guideline when making your selections:

- 📷 How many people will you be cooking for?

- 📷 How many days will you be camping?

- 📷 How many kids will join the group?

- 📷 How many coolers will you have access to?

- 📷 What time of day will you arrive?

- 📷 What time of day will you depart?

- 📷 What activities are planned each day, and how long will they last?

- 📷 What time does everyone wake up?

- 📷 What time does everyone go to bed?

- 📷 Does anyone have a special diet?

These are questions that can help you make up your mind as to what kind of menu you might want to put together for the trip.

Plan for 1½ servings per adult and ½ serving per child, but remember that it is better to have leftovers than to run out of food when you are out in the middle of nowhere. Kids won't always eat what you make, so always have a couple of packages of hot dogs available. Surprisingly, a lot of our recipes have been devoured by kids whose parents said there is no way they will eat that, but it's better safe than sorry.

Once you know everyone's arrival time you can make a plan for the first meal. If you are coming in late, then make it an easy recipe that doesn't require a lot of prep or cook time. Even having it precooked and ready to serve when you arrive is better than eating at eleven o'clock at night.

What time will you check out from the campsite and

leave to head back home? Keep that in mind when planning your last meal, because you still need to break down your camp and hookup. Pat likes to make breakfast burritos the night before an early departure, and just wrap them up in foil and reheat them the next morning on the grill or in the microwave inside the trailer. No cleanup, no prep, and it's delicious. If you have a little more time, you can make the Kitchen Sink Breakfast (page 44) with the leftovers from your previous days of camping.

Some campers get up at 6:00 A.M., and others, like Pat and his wife, like to roll out around 10:00 A.M. on most mornings. This kind of schedule can wreak havoc on any camp chef, so scheduling around this takes planning and good timing. The same applies to the time everyone hits the sack as well.

If you've got vegetarians in your group, good luck! You may need to plan special dishes they can eat. We always tell them we don't like to cross contaminate healthy bland crap with my good meats. Typically, people with special diets bring their own food, so most of them often travel with soy burgers and tofu dogs.

Once you have your numbers in order and the days counted, simply write out the meals and all the ingredients that go along with them and stick to the list. Consider how much food your coolers will hold and pack accordingly. Freeze any food you plan to serve later in the week and use that to help keep your other food ice cold. Remember to keep your meats separated from your vegetables, and always keep your drinks and mixing ice separate from food. Most important, relax and have fun!

19

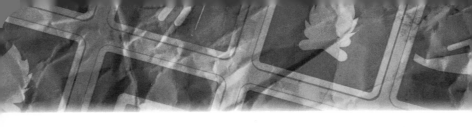

Packing the Cooler

ack your cooler correctly and you will make it last; pack it wrong and you will lose a lot of food. Getting the right cooler will help. We suggest you stick with the thick-sided ones with good thick lids. The body-sized coolers are the best way to go because they hold more ice and product and sometimes you can go an entire weekend with one cooler.

Prep your coolers before each trip in the summer by acclimating them. Put them in your basement or in another cool area for at least forty-eight hours with the lids open before you pack them. If you take the coolers from the warm heated garage during the summer and load them with ice right away it will take at least four bags of ice to cool it off to an optimal temperature.

If you have a big group and lots of different ingredients, separate your coolers according to food groups: beer and drinking ice in one, raw meats in a smaller one, and perishables and produce in another. Keep your produce separated from direct contact with your ice. We put a thick towel between the ice and produce sometimes, which helps keep the ice insulated as well.

Once you are in camp, put your coolers at a slight incline and leave the valves open on the bottoms so the water can drain downhill away from the food to help keep the ice from melting faster. Keep your coolers in the shade all day if you can, which will help keep your ice longer. We look for areas covered by heavy tree limbs and put a tarp above the cooler or around the sides, creating a shaded spot from sunrise to sunset.

The best way to pack dry ice is in the bottom of the cooler. Lay a thin layer of

cardboard on top and a beach towel over that, then layer your ice on the towel. You will be surprised how long it will last. Some campers even fill a body cooler with dry ice on the bottom, followed by cardboard and bags of ice on top to fill up the rest of the cooler. Then they have access to ice the entire trip to refill all their other coolers.

Freezing your meats and packing them on the bottom of your coolers will help keep your ice fresh, but make sure all food products are in resealable plastic bags to help prevent soggy food a few days into a trip. The two-gallon size by Ziploc® is very handy for eighteen-pack egg cartons. We have all experienced the soggy, broken-down, paper egg cartons in the melted ice before, but we continue to pack it because we forget.

Tips for Keeping Your Camp Kitchen Clean

clean kitchen is a workable kitchen, and cooking at a campground makes that job more of a challenge than ever. The first rule of thumb is to try to separate your cooking area from your gathering area.

The picnic tables in a campground have more bacteria on them than a discount motel bedspread. After you remove the pine needles and dead bugs from the table, wipe it down with antibacterial wipes and then cover it with a disposable tablecloth. This will make it safer—and more inviting to use at mealtime.

Always keep a box of disposable latex food-handling gloves in the kitchen to keep down the spread of bacteria and to help keep you from coming into contact with raw meats. If you're working with perishable, uncooked foods, the gloves help protect your fellow campers. And the proctologist joke Pat tells never gets old!

A good handwashing station consists of hand

The Dos and Don'ts of Dealing with a Bear in Camp

My wife and I have put in a lot of time camping over the years, and our favorite spot has a few bear visitors every year. No, not Yogi, Boo-Boo, or Smokey, either. Coming into contact with a large animal three times your size that is scared of you can play tricks with your mind.

One evening my wife went back to our trailer early in the evening, leaving me at a friend's campfire to consume more beverages. It was dark and my wife had taken the only flashlight back with her, leaving me to navigate in the dark wooded campground. I started my trek back to camp taking small steps, trying to find my way.

I rounded the corner to the road to our camp spot, which was partially lit by the moonlight, and I saw another camper walking toward me without a flashlight. As he got closer, I realized it wasn't another camper, but a very large dog with a huge butt and distinct swagger. As we got even closer, I suddenly realized it wasn't a big dog with a large booty, but a small black bear.

Our eyes met and we both stopped cold in our tracks. There were only twenty feet between us. A large truck turned the corner with its headlights catching both of our eyes. I was able to assess his size and came to the conclusion that no matter how much tequila I had had I would not be able to take that guy. Luckily for me the screech that came from my mouth (followed by a loss of bodily functions) scared the bear so much that he bolted from the scene.

A lady from the truck jumped out and screamed, "Did you see that?"

I said, "Can you smell me? Of course I saw that!"

I ran to the trailer, hoping the bear had left the area, and tried to open the door, but my wife had locked it. Being the outdoor adventurer who fears nothing, I started pounding on the door and screaming like a girl, "Let me in!"

I told my wife how I had come face to face with this mammoth creature and how I stood my ground puffing out my chest, risking my life to battle this bear. I know my story changed a little but it's my story. This excited my wife to the point that she wanted to go see the bear for herself. So we grabbed our night vision goggles, flashlight, and some courage and set out for a bear hunt.

I took my wife back to the scene of the encounter, which I thought would be hard to find in the pitch dark, but the smell I left behind was still there and marked the spot. That is when we ran into the park ranger, who was out doing her rounds, and we told her what had happened. She asked what we were doing out there. After hearing ourselves say out loud that we were hunting bear with goggles and a flashlight, we decided it was time to call it a night!

—**Pat**

your clean surfaces overnight. Lay out raw foods on separate fresh sheets of aluminum foil to keep the possibilities of cross contamination to a minimum; you can recycle the aluminum foil afterward.

sanitizer, wet wipes, and antibacterial soap placed next to jugs of water and paper towels. If you are a real clean freak you can always get a thermal jug with a water dispenser and keep it filled with boiled water for hand washing, but the bathroom facilities at the campgrounds will often work just fine.

Keep antibacterial wipes in the kitchen at all times and wipe everything down after working on food prep. Pat even cleans again the next morning because pollen from the trees can land on

For a proper cleanup, wash the dishes by boiling water and filling three wash bins. The first bin should have antibacterial soap, the second bin plain hot water for rinsing, and the third bin should have hot water plus one cap of bleach for a sanitizing rinse. Use paper towels to lay clean dishes on and to dry off afterward. Wet dishes will attract the dirt and dust you kick up from the ground, so it is best to dry dishes immediately.

Shoebox-sized plastic bins with lids are a great place to store your clean utensils because you can close the lid to keep everything sanitary. Keeping your pots and pans inside a larger rubber or plastic container

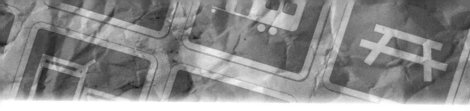

after cleaning will help protect them from kicked-up dirt. If you feel any of these items are contaminated, no need to rewash. Just wipe off with an antibacterial wipe.

Here is a checklist of handy items that will help you keep your kitchen clean:

- Antibacterial wipes
- Disposable tablecloths
- Antibacterial hand soap
- Wet wipes
- Sanitizer
- Antibacterial dish soap
- Nonlatex food handling gloves
- Aluminum foil
- Disposable wash pads
- Clean wash towels
- Large pot for boiling water
- Three washbasin tubs
- Bleach

If You Build It They Will Eat!

 etting up camp has been a longtime tradition of separating the expert camper from the rookie. A rookie will drop chairs, pile everything into one spot, and be disorganized the entire weekend. An expert has a plan before he or she drops the first tarp or piles the wood under the heaviest layered pine tree. Then there are camp chefs who pride themselves on building a complete kitchen outside with everything from a gas-fueled margarita blender to the kitchen sink. Pat happens to be one of those chefs.

His outdoor kitchen consists of a GSI camp table with two extensions, two sinks, and a gray water drain. He sets up two eight-foot folding tables to square the kitchen off, a three-burner Camp Chef grill with the alternative grill box and griddle, a propane blender, a Sunbeam portable propane grill to use as a warmer, and a collapsible shelf that hangs from the outdoor screen room that encloses my kitchen.

A cupboard holds all the spices, oils, paper plates, and

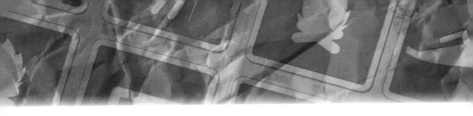

canned food. One of the eight-foot tables acts as a bar and the other is a food prep area and serving station. Pat leaves two body coolers under each table. One is stocked with beer, ice, and soft drinks; the other with perishable foods. Pat keeps a thermometer in the food one to ensure optimal temperature during the weekend.

The two extensions off the GSI table are wire racks. One is used for drying and storing all the pots and pans. The other is for a backup grill warmer. Under the racks are two plastic tubs of kitchen utensils and cleaning supplies.

One propane tank with a dual hose runs all the equipment. The Dutch ovens go inside a gutted-out hibachi with heat-resistant legs placed on one of the tables. Setup time for this project is thirty minutes or two beers!

In the past Pat's wife has observed grown men turn their camp chairs toward us and watch like spectators at a sporting event. When he is finished other campers come over and ask if they can look at the kitchen, and Pat is not ashamed when another guy asks to see

his equipment; in fact, it's a compliment that Pat has more toys than the other guy does, and therefore Pat wins.

Camp friends who show up for trips tease Pat about my setup until he feeds them, and then they shut up! If you build it, they will eat!

Dutch Oven Basics

ost campers seem to be intimidated by the Dutch oven. This is okay. We were those people when we first started camping and we can tell you from experience that if you burn the first three recipes then you become an expert. So let's get down to Dutch oven basics.

The Dutch ovens that we use are cast-iron Lodge brand with tripod legs and lipped-edge lids. We like to use Dutch oven aluminum inserts or aluminum foil on the bottom, which helps with cleanup. We cook with the Dutch oven in two ways: on the ground or in a gutted-out hibachi with no vents on the bottom and heat-resistant legs. This allows you to cook the Dutch oven on top of the table.

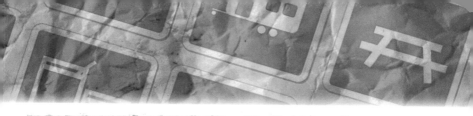

The main tools you'll need are long-handled tongs for handling hot coals and thick welding gloves sold with Dutch oven accessories. To start the coals, use a chimney stack with a space on the bottom for newspaper. Pat always places the stack filled with coals directly on the stovetop and runs the flame at high heat for three minutes to ignite the coals. Then he turns off the flame and lets it sit for five minutes while all the coals ignite themselves. The hibachi comes in handy to keep you off the ground and keep the ground dust from getting in your recipe when you lift the lid.

How the Dutch oven works: When you put your coals on top and around the bottom of the Dutch oven you create a vacuum seal that creates a convection oven inside your Dutch oven. If you run coals on the top only, you will only heat the ingredients on top of the recipe. Same for the bottom.

Coal placement is the key to a good Dutch oven. Never put coals directly under your Dutch oven unless you want to scorch the ingredients under the coals. Instead, place your coals around the edge of the bottom of the Dutch oven in a circular pattern, which allows the heat to run up the sides, helping to distribute it. A good rule of thumb is to take the number of coals around the bottom and double it for the top. Lay your coals on the top

lid around the edge to help distribute the heat down. This creates the convection oven.

We like to run the Dutch oven at 425°F, so we place eight coals around the bottom and sixteen coals on top, depending on the elevation. When you lift the lid to check a recipe you can expect to lose 100° to 125°F, so try not to lift the lid too often. After the recipe reaches its recommended cooking time, if you need to keep it heated for a while you can remove all the coals except three around the bottom and three on the top. This will allow the heat to continue but the dish won't be so hot it overcooks.

If a recipe includes bread on the bottom, try placing a pie tin upside down under the bread, allowing a little space between the bread and the direct heat of the coals, and creating a little room for more air flow.

Keeping Yourself Safe

When you light the grill for your marinated steaks or the Dutch oven and they have reached the optimal temperature, the food will carry an aroma around the camp like it would in a good restaurant kitchen. With a good wind that scent will lift into the tree line up the mountainside and attract the . . . BEARS!

The best way to keep yourself safe when you are spicing up your camp feast is to put the leftover food in your neighbor's campsite! You weren't happy with them anyway. They showed up late last night and made a lot of noise. They left the diesel truck running until 2:00 A.M., and you couldn't fall asleep until 3:00 A.M.

One common mistake made by the species of male who feel more powerful if we are holding a pair of tongs and a beer is wearing the same flannel shirt for five days straight while standing in front of a smoking grill. At the end of the day, you smell like a Burger King employee. The bear smells your clothing when you go to bed wearing it (or when you place that old flannel shirt next to you) and eventually you wake up next to a hairy smelly creature. Instead, use an apron or cooking jacket (e.g., another flannel shirt) that you can take off at the end of your cooking detail and put in the kids' tent so they can have a good story to tell when they grow up. Seriously, put it as far away from your sleeping quarters as possible or in a sealed container.

APPETIZERS

Cheesy Garlic Bread

Serves 4 to 6

1 (16-ounce) large French bread

1 cup mayonnaise

2 tablespoons chopped garlic

½ cup grated Parmesan cheese

Salt and black pepper

Take a loaf of French bread and cut it in half evenly along the long side.

In a medium bowl, combine the mayonnaise, garlic, cheese, and salt and pepper and mix for about 2 minutes. With a rubber spatula, spread the mixture evenly along the cut sides of the bread. Make sure to cover the entire surface so all the bread becomes crispy when you toast it in the Dutch oven.

Place the bread in a Dutch oven, cover it, and put 8 coals on the top and 4 coals around the outside of the bottom (not underneath). You want the heat coming from the top and not so much from the bottom so the bread doesn't burn the bottom and there is an even toasting on top. Cook for 20 minutes, or until nicely browned around the edges.

Brie Cheese Wrap

Serves 4 to 6

1 (8-ounce) can crescent rolls (we prefer Pillsbury)

1 block (0.5 to 0.9 pound) Brie cheese

This is a great starter for a meal. It's also a cool appetizer that wows people by how delicious it looks.

Take the crescent rolls and lay them out flat on a piece of foil. Lay your Brie cheese block on top of the rolls and fold the rolls over the cheese to completely cover every inch of it. If need be, rip pieces of the crescent roll off and cover the exposed areas with them.

Lay the covered cheese in your Dutch oven, cover, and place 8 coals on the top and 4 coals around the outside of the bottom (not underneath). Cook for 20 to 30 minutes, or until the crescent roll crust has browned up nice and crispy.

Sleeping Bag Jalapeños

Serves 6 to 8

1 pound sweet maple sausage

2 (8-ounce) packages cream cheese

½ cup shredded mozzarella cheese

15 to 20 jalapeños, halved and seeded

In a large sauté pan on a medium flame, cook the sausage all the way through until there is no pink left. Add the cream cheese and mozzarella and cook, stirring constantly, for about 7 minutes, or until the cheese is completely melted.

Stuff each jalapeño with about 1 tablespoon of the sausage and cheese mixture. Place the stuffed jalapeños on a grill and cook on low direct heat for 15 minutes. If the grill is not available, you can bake these for 20 minutes in a covered Dutch oven with 8 coals on top and 6 around the outside of the bottom (not underneath).

ENTRÉES

Breakfast

Salmon Benedict

Serves 4 to 6

½ pound cooked salmon (left over from your Dill Salmon recipe the night before, page 118)

4 to 6 slices Canadian bacon

8 tablespoons (1 stick) unsalted butter

¼ cup 2% milk

1 (0.9 ounce, 25 grams) packet hollandaise sauce mixture (we prefer Knorr)

2 large eggs

6 English muffins, halved

Salt and black pepper

Take your leftover salmon, put it in some foil, and reheat it on the grill or griddle. While you're at it, heat up the Canadian bacon, too.

To make your hollandaise sauce, combine the butter, milk, and hollandaise mixture in a medium-sized pan over medium heat. Let this simmer until thick and ready.

Crack your eggs on a hot griddle and let them cook until sunny-side up. You may want to pour a little water on the griddle and cover it so the steam helps cook the eggs to over easy without having to flip them.

Toast your English muffins on the grill. Put your eggs, salmon, and Canadian bacon on one side of each muffin, then drizzle the hollandaise sauce across the top and top with the other half of the muffin. Season with salt and pepper to taste.

This is a traditional breakfast that most people are intimidated by in the woods. This is also a great way to take leftover food from the night before and use it as a breakfast protein.

Dutch Oven Benedict

Serves 4 to 6

1 (16.3-ounce) can biscuits (we prefer Pillsbury)

8 large eggs

6 slices (3 ounces) prosciutto, and/or 6 slices
(3 ounces) pancetta

½ cup shredded Parmesan cheese

Salt and black pepper

Spray your Dutch oven insert with
cooking spray, then place your
separated biscuits on the bottom.
Press your thumb in the middle of
the biscuit to create a biscuit cup,
if you would. Crack an egg in each
biscuit cup, then place some prosciutto and/or pancetta across the
egg. Spread a healthy portion of
Parmesan cheese across the whole
thing. This will create the cheese
sauce that will hold everything together, kind of like glue. Season
with salt and pepper.

Place the insert into the Dutch oven, making sure there is separa-
tion between the bottom of the Dutch oven and the biscuits. We
like to take an unused aluminum pie tin turned upside down and
place it under the insert to create a more indirect heat from the
hot coals. Cover the Dutch oven and place only about 8 coals on
top and 4 coals around the outside of the bottom (not underneath).
Cook for 30 minutes, or until the cheese has melted. Make sure
to keep a close eye on this recipe, because with all those delicate
ingredients it's very sensitive.

Irish Tacos

Serves 6 to 8

1 (2½- to 3-pound) corned beef brisket

8 red potatoes, finely chopped

3 tablespoons olive oil

½ cup chopped white onion

3 cloves garlic, chopped

3 sprigs rosemary, chopped

3 tablespoons chopped fresh thyme

6 to 8 large eggs

6 to 8 flour tortillas

Salt and black pepper

In a large pot, boil the corned beef in water for 1 hour and 30 minutes. Move the meat to a plate and set it aside to cool. Cook the red potatoes in the same water for 8 minutes, then strain them out and rinse them with cold water. This process can be done the night before. Just make sure you leave the potatoes in water overnight or the potatoes will brown from the exposure to oxygen.

Place the olive oil in a skillet or on a griddle over medium-high heat and sauté the onion and garlic until transparent, 3 to 5 minutes. Add the potatoes and heat together for 15 minutes. Chop the corned beef into small pieces and add it to the mix. Add the rosemary and thyme and cook for 10 minutes.

Scramble the eggs, add the corned beef hash, and place the mixture on grilled tortillas. Season with salt and pepper to taste.

Omelet in a Bag

Serves 4 to 6

8 large eggs

½ cup 2% milk

½ cup chopped onion

½ cup chopped green bell pepper

½ cup chopped button mushrooms

½ cup chopped zucchini

½ cup chopped yellow squash

Salt and black pepper

This is a favorite while camping because it's easy and there's no cleanup! You can add other vegetables you may enjoy as well.

Whip the eggs and milk together, then divide the mixture among 4 to 6 (1-gallon) resealable plastic bags. Add a few tablespoons of vegetables to each bag. Salt and pepper to your liking, then seal the bags shut.

Fill a large pot about three-quarters full with water and bring it to a boil over high heat. Drop the bags in the water and cook for about 15 minutes, or until the eggs are firm. Check often because it may take longer for each omelet to cook depending on the amount of eggs and ingredients. When the omelets are firm to the touch, pull them out and serve.

Note: There is no meat in this recipe, but we do not endorse that at all. You can add bacon, sausage, ham, or any other meat you prefer. But some people enjoy all vegetables, which makes a good omelet for those who are watching their weight.

Stuffed French Toast

Serves 4 to 6

1 (21-ounce) can apple pie filling

1 large (16-ounce) loaf French bread

6 large eggs

½ cup 2% milk

1 tablespoon ground cinnamon, plus more for sprinkling

½ teaspoon ground nutmeg

1 tablespoon vanilla extract

2 tablespoons sugar

1 (8-ounce) container nondairy whipped topping (we prefer Cool Whip)

Maple syrup, for serving

This is a great way to start your day every day and people will think you're a master cook because of how beautiful this recipe turns out.

Pour the apple pie filling into a small saucepan and set it over low heat to warm up while you work on the French toast.

Cut your French bread into slices approximately ¾ inch thick and set them aside. In a medium bowl, whip together the eggs, milk, cinnamon, nutmeg, and vanilla extract. This is called an egg wash. Take your French bread slices and dip them into the egg wash, making sure all surfaces of the bread are soaked without drowning the bread, either. You want just enough egg wash for all the flavors to adhere to the surface of the bread.

Now lay your bread on a griddle or sauté pan on medium heat, making sure to use nonstick spray so there's no sticking. Sprinkle a little of the sugar and some cinnamon on the surfaces of the bread as it cooks. Once the bottom sides are golden brown, flip them over and cook the other side until golden brown; this usually takes about 5 minutes. Once the French toast is cooked, lay one slice on a plate and spoon a layer of the apple pie filling over it. Lay another piece of French toast on top of that, then put a heaping amount of whipped topping on top. Sprinkle a little more cinnamon on everything and you're done! Serve with maple syrup.

Kitchen Sink Breakfast

Serves 6 to 8

Everything left over from the week of cooking (vegetables, meats, bread—whatever you've got—make sure your vegetables are chopped into bite-sized pieces)

2 cups shredded cheese (cheddar, mozzarella, provolone, for example, or a mixture)

8 large eggs

1 cup 2% milk

Exactly what it says, the kitchen sink breakfast is a combination of leftover food from your camping trip. Place your leftovers (ham, cooked bacon, sausage, potatoes, bread, onions, peppers, mushrooms, and even seasonings) in a Dutch oven insert. Sprinkle all the cheeses that are left over as well over the top of everything. Whip the eggs with the milk, then pour it over the top. Put the insert into the Dutch oven, cover it, and place 10 coals around the top edge and 6 coals around the outside of the bottom (not underneath). Cook for 30 minutes, or until the eggs are completely cooked through. You've got yourself a tasty and easy recipe you can serve anytime during the day!

It's Not A Competition!

Cooking for large or small groups can be fun and entertaining. For Pat it's always been about making people happy and letting food bring people together.

For some reason campers feel like they need to compete with you when it comes to cooking. Most camps will split up meals and duties to offset the cost of the weekend and not every group will have camp chefs in them. This can result in some feeling like they don't want to be a part of the group because they can't compete. Just simply ask the nearest camp chef for help and he or she will most likely offer to cook for you or, even better, let you use their setup.

I can't tell you how many people have bought one of our videos and said, "I can't wait to show up our camp chef now. He thinks he has the best Dutch oven recipes." For the record, if you own our DVD and this cookbook, you are now that camp chef everyone is trying to beat.

The most productive camp cooking weekends are the ones when two people are in charge of the menu. The more people involved in the process, the more complicated it gets, and things get missed. Keep it simple, campers, and designate two chefs to be in charge. These two can delegate prep jobs if they like. My wife doesn't like to cook but always does the cleanup because she appreciates the time I put into cooking.

There are three different ways to plan a successful weekend:

1. The camp chef assigns a mealtime and day to each couple or pair of friends. Those people are in charge of cooking that meal or shopping for the designated chef, so he or she can cook it.

2. The designated camp chef plans the meals and assigns a shopping list to each group. Those people are in charge of bringing those foods for the meal or meals.

3. Let your camp chef plan the meals and shop for all the in-gredients, then everyone pays the camp chef back at the beginning of the trip.

backpack (*chiefly US*), daypack (*US*), rucksack (*chiefly Brit*)

air mattress, air bed

Three-Marinade Skewers

Serves 4 to 6

10 wooden skewers

Beef

2 pounds USDA choice steak tips, cubed

1 (16-ounce) bottle Italian dressing
(we prefer Ken's Steak House)

Chicken

2 to 3 (1- to 1½-pound) boneless skinless
chicken breasts, cubed

1 (12-ounce) can mango nectar
(we prefer Kern's)

2 sprigs tarragon, chopped

2 basil leaves, chopped

2 tablespoons chopped garlic

Salt and black pepper

Scallops

3 tablespoons lemon juice

2 tablespoons lemon pepper seasoning

1 tablespoon all-purpose flour

1 pound whole jumbo sea scallops

Salt and black pepper

Vegetables

5 pieces white onion, chopped, for each kabob

2 whole button mushrooms for each kabob

4 pieces green bell pepper, cut into chunks, for each kabob

Place 10 wooden skewers in a 1-gallon resealable plastic bag, fill it with enough water to cover them, seal it tightly, and let the skewers soak for 4 to 5 hours. This helps prevent the skewers from burning when they are being grilled.

Place the steak tips in a 1-gallon resealable plastic bag, then empty the entire bottle of Italian dressing into the bag. Seal the bag tightly and squeeze to mix. Let this sit in a cooler or refrigerator for 10 hours.

Place your cubed chicken in a 1-gallon resealable plastic bag, then add the mango nectar, tarragon, basil, and garlic. Seal the bag tightly and squeeze to mix. Let this sit in a cooler or refrigerator for 8 hours.

In a small bowl, mix together the lemon juice and lemon pepper seasoning, then add the flour gradually until the marinade thickens a bit. Place the scallops in a 1-gallon resealable plastic bag and pour in the marinade. Seal the bag tightly and squeeze to mix. Let this sit in a cooler or refrigerator for 5 to 6 hours.

Divide the marinated meat, poultry, and fish and the vegetables evenly among the skewers. Grill until the meat, poultry, and fish are thoroughly cooked.

Notes: Some meats take longer to cook or may be larger than another cut of meat on your kabob, so take that into consideration when grilling your skewers.

These skewers are great with rice pilaf or Dirty Rice on page 148.

Asian Lettuce Wraps

Serves 4 to 6

4 boneless skinless chicken breasts
(2½ to 3 pounds)

2 tablespoons sesame oil

½ cup chopped yellow onion

2 cloves garlic, chopped

2 tablespoons soy sauce

½ cup teriyaki marinade

2 tablespoons sweet red chili sauce

2 tablespoons toasted sesame seeds

½ cup chopped green onion

2 heads romaine lettuce

½ cup chow mein noodles

In a saucepan over medium heat, boil the chicken breasts for 20 minutes. When cool, dice the chicken and set it aside.

Heat the sesame oil in a skillet over medium heat and sauté the yellow onion and garlic for 3 to 4 minutes, then add the diced chicken, soy sauce, teriyaki marinade, and chili sauce and simmer for 10 minutes over medium heat. Add the sesame seeds and green onion and toss to mix; take it off the heat.

Pull the leaves off of the heads of romaine lettuce. Put a scoop of the mixture into the cupped portion of each of the leaves, sprinkle chow mein noodles on top, wrap, and serve.

This can also be served in bowls with a side of rice noodles or crunchy chow mein noodles.

Ponderosa Steak Sandwich

Serves 4 to 6

2 tablespoons olive oil

½ cup chopped white onion

2 tablespoons chopped garlic

⅓ cup sliced button mushrooms

Salt and black pepper

2 (1- to 1½-pound) rib eye steaks

2 tablespoons mixed grill seasoning

3 tablespoons red wine vinegar

⅓ cup teriyaki marinade

4 large hoagie buns

6 slices provolone cheese

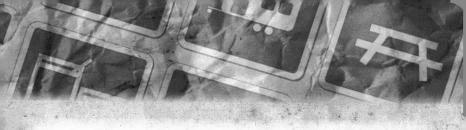

This sandwich is named after the state park it was invented in, Ponderosa State Park, in McCall, Idaho.

Heat the olive oil in a sauté pan over medium heat and saute the onion, garlic, and mushrooms until fully cooked, 5 to 7 minutes. Season with salt and pepper.

Sear the rib eye steaks on each side on a hot grill, grinding some mixed grill seasoning on them as they cook. This should take 5 to 7 minutes total. Once the rib eyes are cooked to medium rare, pull them off the grill and cut them up into thin slices about ⅓ inch thick.

Put the sautéed vegetables and slices of steak in a large sauté pan and sauté over medium heat for 3 minutes. Add your red wine vinegar and teriyaki marinade and cook for about 5 more minutes. Make sure the steak doesn't overcook as you want it still medium rare to medium when it's done.

Take your hoagie buns and lay a few slices of provolone cheese across the openings. Throw them on the grill until the cheese melts across the bun. Once both the steak and buns are ready, lay the buns open-faced on a plate, then place the grilled steak across the provolone on the bun and let that melt into each other. This will finish the melting process for the cheese and mix all the flavors together to make a hearty sandwich before you go for a hike.

VISION QUEST

When you get to be my age and married for ten years you start to use selective hearing and your brain reflexes get slower. I tend to just say, "Yes," when my wife says, "I have a great idea. It will be good for us, and we can learn a lot about ourselves." Nodding, "Uhhha, sure, wait, what?"

Too late, I was already signed up for a yearlong study of the Native American spiritual culture using a shaman and sweat lodges, with a graduation test at the end called a Vision Quest. During this quest you spend four days alone in the woods with little water and a handful of food. Why does my wife get attracted to these kinds of things, you ask? Because she hates me!

Actually, I really did enjoy spending time with my fellow questers and our shaman. Learning the culture and spiritual beliefs was the most enlightening experience of my life, and the four days of mountain solitude were educational and profound.

Each classmate was given a specific abandoned area to set up camp and a strict diet to help enhance the experience. I was assigned an all-fruit diet. I was supposed to eat only one orange for breakfast and an apple for dinner each day the entire trip. I also snuck in some dried

fruit, but it didn't fare well in the constant downpour over the four days. For the record, fresh fruit daily sounds delicious, nutritious, and good for you. However, your body does weird things and you end up digging a lot of holes.

We were set up at 9,000 feet in the mountains during the month of May in Idaho. Each of us was alone and not allowed to speak to anyone if you saw them. There was still snow on the ground, the rain was constant, the daily high was 38°F, and my schedule was to be awake every two hours for four days straight.

Being accustomed to a comfortable trailer with Pottery Barn colors, a down comforter, and a giant outdoor kitchen with a gourmet menu, I was pissed. The only vision I received was a dream of corned beef hash and eggs, biscuits and gravy, a big fat mug of coffee, and real toilet paper!

I missed the comforts of my trailer, my flat-screen TV and surround sound, and lying in bed with my wife during thunderstorms. I did, however, learn that those moments should be cherished and not taken for granted, and to step outside and enjoy what Mother Nature is giving us to observe, hear, and smell. See, my shaman did teach me something.

I also learned the answer to that great question: Does a bear shit in the woods? Yes, in the middle of my camp, and he didn't even bother to bury it!

—**Pat**

Camp Calzone

Serves 4 to 6

Sauce

1 (12-ounce) can tomato paste

1 (14-ounce) can tomato puree

1 tablespoon chopped garlic

1 tablespoon Italian seasoning

1 (13.8-ounce) can pizza dough

All-purpose flour, for spreading the dough

Fillings

1 green bell pepper, seeded and chopped

½ white onion, chopped

8 button mushrooms, quartered

1 cup mozzarella cheese

1 cup 3-cheese blend (mozzarella, cheddar, Jack)

½ cup pepperoni slices (see Note)

Mix the tomato paste, tomato puree, garlic, and Italian seasoning in a bowl. Spread the pizza dough out on some foil, using a little flour to keep it from sticking if necessary. Cut the dough into portion sizes to fit your appetite. Spread the sauce on the pieces of dough, making sure not to get near the edges. Add your fillings, spreading them evenly along the dough, again staying away from the edges. Fold each piece of dough over the toppings, pinching the edges together to seal them.

Place the calzones in a Dutch oven insert, then in the Dutch oven, cover it, and cook for 20 minutes with 12 coals around the top edge and 6 coals around the outside of the bottom (not underneath), until the crust is golden brown or the cheeses inside are completely melted.

Note: You may add any meats and vegetables you want to your calzone. These are just suggestions.

How Pat's Mind Works

Most camper and outdoor enthusiasts will put together a list of activities and sights to see while camping. Some will load the bike rack on top of their truck or the back of the rig, all for a weekend of mountain recreational action. Some will concentrate on loading the boat with all the right fishing equipment or water bottles and backpacks for the day hikes they have planned. All those activities normally start early in the morning and require motivation, a group effort, and an agreement with fellow campers.

As for me, before a trip all I can think about is what will go with salmon and how I can use red potato leftovers for breakfast. If I start a marinade the night before, how long do I need to soak a chicken? How much fresh rosemary should I pack and what will I wrap the asparagus in to keep it fresh? While others seek the excitement of adventure and physical fitness, I think and dream of food. I can walk into the grocery store with no list or idea of what I am making and within five minutes I have created an entire main course using the first item that jumps out at me in the produce or meat departments.

Not that there is anything wrong with mountain biking, fishing, hiking, and boating. I'd just rather think about how many Dutch ovens I will be using in a three-day period. Or how to break the news to the vegetarian camping with us that tofu is flavored rubber and I just cannot crosscontaminate my vegetables.

Twice-Baked Barbecue Chicken

Serves 4 to 6

2½ to 4 pounds chicken thighs and legs, bone-in or boneless

2 tablespoons chopped garlic

½ white onion, chopped

1 (12-ounce) bottle barbecue sauce (we prefer Sweet Baby Ray's)

⅓ cup firmly packed brown sugar

Salt and black pepper

Prepare your Dutch oven insert with a little nonstick spray. Take your chicken pieces and lay them in the insert. Throw some chopped garlic and onion on top, then pour the barbecue sauce over everything, sprinkle the brown sugar on top, and salt and pepper to your liking. Place the insert into the Dutch oven, cover it, and put about 12 coals around the top edge and 8 coals around the outside of the bottom (not underneath). Cook for about 45 minutes to an hour, or until the chicken is fully cooked.

Take the chicken out of the Dutch oven and lay it on a hot grill for 7 to 10 minutes. This makes the chicken so tender it just falls off the bone. Make sure after it cooks for the second time that you serve it in the sauce you originally made in the Dutch oven. This ensures the juiciness of the chicken.

Pecan-Crusted Chicken

Serves 4 to 6

1 (4-ounce) bag pecans (whole or chopped)

2 large eggs

¼ cup 2% milk

3 tablespoons unsalted butter

4 (1½- to 2-pound) boneless skinless chicken breasts

Salt and black pepper

Chop up your pecans very finely and lay them nicely on a flat plate or surface.

In a medium bowl, whip together the eggs and milk. This is called an egg wash. It's used to help flavors or ingredients stick to meats. It's also good for sealing envelopes if you don't like licking them. (Joking—don't try that at home!)

Melt the butter in a sauté pan over medium heat. Take a chicken breast and dip it into the egg wash, then move it directly to the chopped pecans, pressing it against the pecans so they adhere to it. Sear the chicken until both sides have a crispy brown cooked coating. This usually takes 7 to 10 minutes. Salt and pepper to your liking.

Take the seared chicken breasts, lay them in a Dutch oven insert, and put the insert into the Dutch oven. Cover it and put 12 coals on top and 6 coals around the outside of the bottom (not underneath). Let the dish cook for about 35 minutes, or until the chicken is completely finished, no pink. This depends on the thickness of the chicken breasts, so be very careful not to overcook or undercook the chicken, unless your mother-in-law is coming for dinner, then either overcook or undercook the chicken not to her liking!

This dish is best served with the Parmesan Cheese Sauce on page 174 or the Dirty Rice on page 148.

Spicy Tequila Chicken

Serves 4 to 6

4 to 6 boneless skinless chicken breasts (2½ to 3 pounds)

1½ cups tequila

1 tablespoon horseradish sauce

2 tablespoons soy sauce

¼ cup lime juice

3 tablespoons white wine vinegar

1 tablespoon liquid smoke

Salt and black pepper

Place all the ingredients in a 1- or 2-gallon resealable plastic bag. Seal the bag tightly, squeeze to mix, and marinate for 8 hours. Try not to marinate too much longer than that because it will oversaturate and could spoil the flavor. Cook the chicken on a hot grill for about 7 to 10 minutes, making sure you seal the juices in to ensure the flavors burst when you take your first bite.

Jerk Chicken

Serves 4 to 6

2 teaspoons sugar

1½ teaspoons crushed red pepper flakes

1½ teaspoons onion powder

½ teaspoon ground nutmeg

1 teaspoon black pepper

1 teaspoon ground allspice

⅛ teaspoon ground cloves

½ teaspoon salt

1½ tablespoons ground thyme

4 pounds boneless skinless chicken breasts (you can also use legs and thighs)

Place everything except the chicken in a 1-gallon resealable plastic bag, seal the bag tightly, and squeeze to mix. Throw the chicken in the bag, seal it tightly, and shake until it's well seasoned. Take the chicken out of the bag and throw it on your grill over direct heat until it's fully cooked, 7 to 10 minutes. This recipe is best served with rice pilaf or the Dirty Rice on page 148.

BEAR VS. POP-UP

My favorite camping rig of all time was a pop-up tent trailer with canvas sides and mosquito net windows. It had an aluminum door that slid into place and a hard top to keep you protected from the outside environment. That is, until you woke up to the sounds of something foraging outside under your tent trailer awning.

Early one morning, when the sun was barely creeping over the tree line, I was awakened by a thump. I climbed out of my sleeping rack with the stealthy movement of a slightly oversized gorilla so I wouldn't spook what was out there. I could still hear noises coming from the porch area as I made my way to the door. I slowly opened the door and peeked outside . . . looking . . . looking . . . and there it was, a black bear sniffing around my equipment.

I slammed the door shut hard enough to startle him, but instead of getting scared like most bears, he lumbered over to check out the whimpering noise behind the door. Now I was staring at the curious black bear through the clear vinyl living room window and the bear looked back at me with the same enthusiasm you see in someone at the zoo looking into a cage.

From the bear's point of view I was a poor sap locked up in a small, easily accessible cage. I imagined him wondering, "I sure hope he has enough water and food in there. Is he going to start pacing back and forth in a predictable caged animal pattern of behavior? I wonder if the parks department will get mad if I eat him."

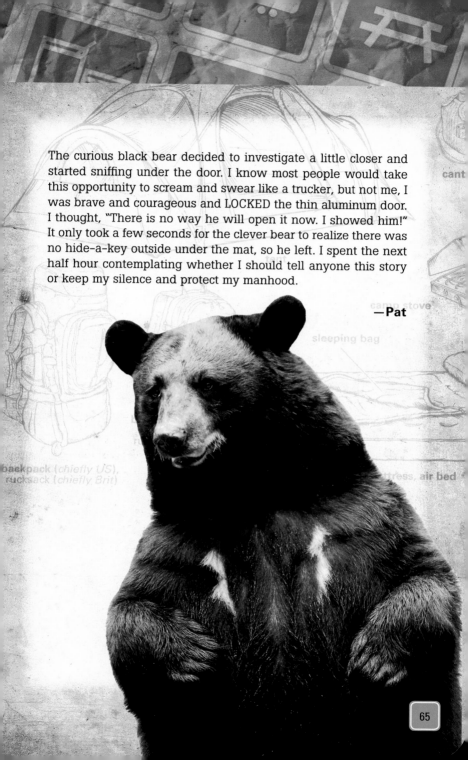

The curious black bear decided to investigate a little closer and started sniffing under the door. I know most people would take this opportunity to scream and swear like a trucker, but not me, I was brave and courageous and LOCKED the thin aluminum door. I thought, "There is no way he will open it now. I showed him!" It only took a few seconds for the clever bear to realize there was no hide-a-key outside under the mat, so he left. I spent the next half hour contemplating whether I should tell anyone this story or keep my silence and protect my manhood.

—**Pat**

Beer-Butted Chicken

Serves 8 to 10

2 (12-ounce) cans beer (we suggest a darker beer with more flavor)

2 whole chickens (4 to 5 pounds each)

½ cup hot sauce (we prefer Frank's RedHot sauce)

1 (12-ounce) bottle barbecue sauce (we prefer Jack's BBQ Sauce)

2 tablespoons barbecue rub (we prefer Billy Bob's BBQ rub seasoning salts)

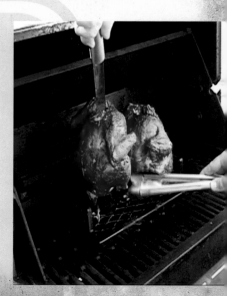

This recipe uses indirect heat to cook the chicken slowly and maintain the juices. Turn the two outside burners of your grill on high heat, leaving the middle burner off.

Open the cans of beer from the top with a can opener so the beer has a chance to boil over and absorb into the meat. Place the cans on the grill or in stands made to hold them (see Note). Take your chickens and place each on top of a can, standing them upright with their backs facing away from each other. This will ensure that the meaty breasts cook slowly.

Put the hot sauce, barbecue sauce, and barbecue rub in a medium bowl and mix well.

Baste the chickens until the entire surfaces are covered with sauce. Continue to baste every 15 to 20 minutes for about 2 hours, or until the chicken is fully cooked. You can use a meat thermometer if you have it; the chicken is done when the internal temperature reaches 180°F. This will ensure that the sauce not only sticks to the chicken, but absorbs into the meat. After a few hours the sauce will begin to thicken and make a crispy layer on the chicken's skin.

Note: Many stores sell stands especially made for making beer-butted chicken. They will hold the cans of beer and allow the chickens to stay upright.

Sweet-and-Sour Chicken

Serves 4 to 6

4 boneless skinless chicken breasts (2½ to 3 pounds) (you can use legs and thighs as well)

1 (16-ounce) bottle Russian salad dressing

1 (1-ounce) packet onion soup mix

⅓ cup soy sauce

9 ounces (half a jar) apricot preserves

Salt and black pepper

This is a recipe you can put in the Dutch oven, go for a hike and come back, and it will be ready to eat!

Place the chicken on the bottom of a Dutch oven insert, then empty  the entire bottle of Russian dressing over the top, followed by the onion soup mix, the soy sauce, and the apricot preserves. Salt and pepper to your liking, then mix it all up so it cooks evenly.

Lay the insert into the Dutch oven. Put 14 coals around the top edge and 8 coals around the outside of the bottom (not underneath) and cook for 1½ hours, or until there is no pink in the chicken. You may want to check on it on occasion to make sure it's cooking at a nice pace. This will be so tender and full of flavor! When you pick up the chicken it will fall apart.

Dutch-Elatta

Serves 4 to 6

4 boneless skinless chicken breasts (1½ to 2 pounds)

Salt and black pepper

2 (10.75-ounce) cans condensed cream of chicken soup

1 (16-ounce) container sour cream

1 (8-ounce) can diced chiles

2 bunches green onions, diced

2½ cups shredded cheddar cheese

1 (12-ounce) can refried beans

8 large flour tortillas

1 bunch cilantro, chopped

2 plum tomatoes (such as Roma), diced

2 cups chopped lettuce

1 yellow onion, chopped

Cook the chicken in a sauté pan on medium heat for about 10 to 15 minutes, or until the chicken is cooked completely through (no pink inside). Season with salt and pepper. Remove the chicken from the pan, cut it into pieces, and set them aside.

In a medium bowl, mix the cream of chicken soup, sour cream, chiles, green onions, 1 cup of cheddar cheese, and the refried beans. Place a little of the mixture into each tortilla, roll the tortillas, and place them in your Dutch oven insert until it's full. Spread the remaining mixture over the top of the tortillas and sprinkle with the remaining 1½ cups of cheese. Cover the Dutch oven, put 12 coals around the top edge and 6 coals around the outside of the bottom (not underneath), and cook for about 40 minutes, until the cheese on top has melted. After cooking completely, let stand for 5 minutes, then serve with the cilantro, tomatoes, lettuce, and onion on top.

CAN I HELP YOU WITH ANYTHING?

"Can I help you with anything?" is a favorite question fellow campers politely ask while curiously looking at Pat's camp cooking setup. They will soon find themselves elbow deep in chopped onions and shredded lettuce. He never turns down help from anyone in the kitchen! He puts them to work chopping ingredients for upcoming recipes, which keeps him from having to do it himself. This strategy used to work for him when he started out, but now his friends have caught on to his evil plan and they steer clear of him all day at camp while he is inside the kitchen area.

A way to eliminate being avoided by your camp friends is to prechop and dice everything before you leave home, roll it up in resealable plastic bags, and put it in the cooler. The less prep you have to do in camp, the easier it is to concentrate on beverages that need to be consumed.

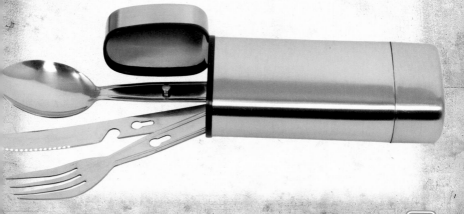

Turmeric Chicken

Serves 4 to 6

3 tablespoons unsalted butter

½ cup chopped yellow onion

1 (3.5-ounce) bag thinly sliced almonds

1 (7.2-ounce) packet rice pilaf

1½ to 2 pounds chicken thighs and legs

3 tablespoons turmeric, or more to your liking

2 (14-ounce) cans chicken broth

Salt and black pepper

Place the butter, onion, almonds, and rice pilaf in your Dutch oven insert and toast on medium-low heat until nice and browned. Put your chicken legs and thighs on top and sprinkle with the turmeric, making sure to cover the chicken as much as possible. You may want to throw in more turmeric for its distinctive flavor depending on your own personal preference. You can always taste it before serving and add a little more turmeric to your liking. Pour the chicken broth over the top, then season with salt and pepper.

Cover the Dutch oven and put 16 coals around the top edge and 10 coals around the outside of the bottom (not underneath). Cook for a good 2 hours, or until the chicken is cooked through. Check on it every once in a while, making sure to stir, to see if the chicken broth is being absorbed and the flavor is mixing well.

Blackened Chicken Pepper Pasta

Serves 4 to 6

½ pound linguine

⅔ cup unsalted butter

2 tablespoons chopped garlic

Salt and black pepper

4 boneless skinless chicken breasts
(1½ to 2 pounds), cubed

2 tablespoons blackened seasoning

1 cup seeded chopped green bell pepper

2 tablespoons olive oil

2 large tomatoes, seeded and chopped

1 to 2 cups heavy whipping cream

½ cup shredded Parmesan cheese

Fill a large pot with lightly salted water and bring to a boil over medium-high heat. Once the water is boiling, stir in the linguine and return to a boil. Cook the linguine, uncovered, until al dente, about 11 minutes. Drain and set aside.

Heat the butter in a large sauté pan over medium heat, then add the garlic, salt, and pepper. Let the garlic cook up for 3 minutes. Add the cubed chicken breast and cook for a few minutes, then season with the blackened seasoning. Continue to sauté until the chicken is almost fully cooked through, about 7 minutes. If you press against the chicken and there's a little softness in the middle, you are ready to continue. You want to make sure that the chicken is nicely blackened.

Add your green pepper and cook until it is softened, about 5 minutes. Then add the olive oil, tomatoes, and cream. Cook until the cream and oil reduce and thicken, about 10 minutes. Then add the Parmesan cheese and cook, stirring, until fully melted. The sauce is done.

Pour the creamy blackened chicken pepper mixture in with the cooked linguine, then mix well so the creamy sauce coats all the pasta to ensure maximum flavor. Salt and pepper to your liking and serve.

Chicken Camp Casserole

Serves 4 to 6

4 (1½- to 2-pound) boneless skinless chicken breasts, cubed

2 (10.75-ounce) cans condensed cream of mushroom soup

1 cup frozen peas

1 sleeve crushed crackers (preferably Ritz)

1½ cups shredded Gruyère cheese

Salt and black pepper

Lay your cubed chicken breasts on the bottom of your Dutch oven insert. Pour the soup on top, then add your peas and the crushed crackers and stir everything up. Sprinkle your Gruyère cheese on top, then salt and pepper to your liking. Place the insert into the Dutch oven, cover it, and put 10 coals around the top edge and 6 coals around the outside of the bottom (not underneath). Make sure to check on this often because you don't want this to cook unevenly. You will know it is done when the crackers brown up and the cheese has melted completely or you can pull out the largest piece of chicken, cut into it, and see if it is completely cooked.

This delicious and easy-to-make recipe was created when Mike was on the road doing stand-up comedy in Chicago. He was staying at my friend Al Stepan's house, and they were stuck inside due to a huge snowstorm. They were hungry and didn't want to order out, so they looked in the cabinets and fridge, came up with these ingredients, and gave it a shot. They were very pleased with how it came out, but even more pleased that they didn't have to spend money and wait for a delivery guy. After a nap, they had seconds, and it was as good as when it first came out of the oven, which is proof that it's a great recipe. So be creative in the kitchen when you are home and don't want to leave. You may serendipitously come up with some awesome recipes. That's how we do it!

Chicken Pot Pie

Serves 4 to 6

1 pound boneless skinless chicken breast halves, cubed

1 cup chopped carrots

1 cup frozen green peas

½ cup sliced celery

⅓ cup unsalted butter

⅓ cup chopped onion

⅓ cup all-purpose flour

Salt and black pepper

¼ teaspoon celery seed

1¾ cups chicken broth

⅔ cup 2% milk

2 (9-inch) unbaked pie crusts

In a large saucepan over medium heat, combine the chicken, carrots, peas, and celery. Add water to cover and boil for 15 minutes. Remove from the heat, drain, and set aside.

In another saucepan over medium heat, melt the butter and cook the onion until soft and translucent, 5 to 7 minutes. Stir in the flour, salt and pepper, and celery seed. Slowly stir in the chicken broth and milk until smooth. Simmer over medium-low heat until thick, about 7 minutes. Remove from the heat and set aside.

Place the chicken mixture in a pie tin that has been layered by a pie crust. Pour the hot liquid mixture into the pie. Cover with the top crust, seal the edges of the top and bottom crusts together, and cut away any excess dough. Make several small slits in the top crust to allow steam to escape.

Place 14 coals on the top and 7 coals around the outside of the bottom (not underneath), and cook for about 45 minutes.

Chicken Spedini

Serves 4 to 6

2 cups Italian seasoned bread crumbs

1 cup grated Romano cheese

Salt and black pepper

1 tablespoon minced fresh parsley

4 cloves garlic, chopped

6 boneless skinless chicken breasts (2½ to 3 pounds), cubed

1 cup olive oil

6 wooden skewers

In a 1-gallon resealable plastic bag, mix the bread crumbs, cheese, salt and pepper, parsley, and garlic. Dip the chicken in ½ cup olive oil, then toss it into the bread crumb mixture. Seal the bag tightly, then shake to coat the chicken.

Remove the chicken from the bag and place it in a large sauté pan over medium heat with ½ cup olive oil in the pan to cook until the chicken is seared and browned on each side, about 7 minutes.

Take the seared chicken cubes and put them on skewers, pushing them close together. Since we are not putting the skewers directly on a flame, there is no need to soak them first in water. Place the skewered chicken in a Dutch oven insert, put it in the Dutch oven, cover it, and put 12 coals around the top edge and 6 coals around the outside of the bottom (not underneath). Cook for about 20 minutes, or until the chicken is completely done. If the chicken breasts are especially thick, you may need to cook them for about 5 minutes more. Serve at once, alone or topped with Amogio Sauce (page 180).

Pat's Biggest Test

My biggest test as a camp chef came when a group of high school friends went to Lake Powell. We spent seven nights camping on a small pontoon houseboat dragging two Jet Skis with six people aboard. The group put me in charge of shopping, cooking, and serving all the meals.

We began the trip in the hot Arizona desert with 100°F temperatures. We had two body coolers, two regular coolers, and a small camp refrigerator; food for twenty-one meals (breakfast, lunch, and dinner); and fifteen cases of beer and ice for mixed drinks. I had a very small kitchen to work in, although I planned the meals so that some of the dinner leftovers would be used in breakfast recipes and some of the leftover breakfasts would carry over into dinner.

We ate gourmet meals every night and had no leftover or spoiled food when we landed. I put everyone on the boat to work on meal prep in the morning and cleaning duties after meals. We would rotate the beer and ice out with the coolers so every cooler was empty at the end of the week. The body coolers had layers of dry ice so the chicken stayed frozen. The greens were eaten early on the trip to avoid spoiling.

I planned steak, chicken, pot roast, specialty salad, and Mexican dishes in the evenings, and egg, pancake, Benedict, and corned beef hash recipes in the mornings. We ate sandwiches and chips every day for lunch.

Most adventure seekers will come away from a weekend like this with a nickname like Champ, Captain, or Master. Not me! "Cookie" was the name I came away with!

Chicken Cacciatore

Serves 4 to 6

1 tablespoon vegetable oil

4 boneless skinless chicken breast halves (2½ to 3 pounds)

1¾ cups chicken broth (we prefer Swanson)

1 teaspoon dried oregano leaves, crushed

1 teaspoon garlic powder

1 small green bell pepper, seeded and cut into 2-inch-long strips

1 (14.5-ounce) can diced tomatoes

1 medium onion, cut into wedges

8 pearl onions

Salt

¼ teaspoon black pepper

2½ cups uncooked medium shell-shaped pasta

Heat the oil in a large sauté pan over medium heat. Add the chicken and cook, turning once, for 10 minutes or until seared on both sides.

Add the broth, oregano, garlic powder, green pepper, diced tomatoes, onions, salt, and black pepper to the pan, stir, and bring to a boil. Stir in the pasta, reduce the heat to low, then cover to allow all the ingredients to absorb the flavors. Cook for about 20 minutes, or until the pasta is al dente.

Chicken Florentine Casserole

Serves 4 to 6

4 to 6 boneless skinless chicken breast halves
(1½ to 2 pounds)

4 tablespoons (½ stick) unsalted butter

3 teaspoons chopped garlic

1 tablespoon lemon juice

1 (10.75-ounce) can condensed
cream of mushroom soup

1 tablespoon Italian seasoning

½ cup heavy whipping cream

½ cup grated Parmesan cheese

2 (13.5-ounce) cans spinach, drained

8 fresh white button mushrooms, sliced

⅔ cup bacon bits from a jar

2 cups shredded mozzarella cheese

Cook the chicken on a grill over direct medium heat until there is no pink left in the middle, 15 to 20 minutes. Remove from the heat and set aside.

Melt the butter in a medium saucepan over medium heat. Stirring constantly, mix in the garlic, lemon juice, soup, Italian seasoning, cream, and Parmesan cheese.

Arrange the spinach over the bottom of your Dutch oven insert. Cover the spinach with the mushrooms. Pour half the mixture from the saucepan over the mushrooms. Arrange the chicken breasts over that, and cover with the remaining sauce mixture. Sprinkle with bacon bits and top with mozzarella cheese.

Put the insert in the Dutch oven, cover it, and put 16 coals around the top edge and 8 coals around the outside of the bottom (not underneath). Cook for about 40 minutes, or until the cheese has browned on the top.

Chicken Cordon Bleu

Serves 4 to 6

6 boneless skinless chicken breast halves (2 to 3 pounds)

6 slices Swiss cheese

6 slices ham (lunch meat style)

3 tablespoons all-purpose flour

1 teaspoon paprika

6 tablespoons unsalted butter

½ cup white wine

1 teaspoon chicken bouillon granules

1 tablespoon cornstarch

1 cup heavy whipping cream

If the chicken breasts are thicker than ½ inch, pound them thinner. Place one slice of cheese and one slice of ham on each breast, leaving ½ inch of space around the edges. Fold the edges of the chicken over the filling and secure them with toothpicks. Mix the flour and paprika in a small bowl and use them to coat the chicken pieces.

Heat the butter in a large skillet over medium-high heat and cook the chicken until browned on all sides. Add the wine and bouillon. Reduce the heat to low, cover, and simmer for 30 minutes, until the chicken is no longer pink and its juices run clear.

Remove the toothpicks and transfer the breasts to a warm platter. Blend the cornstarch with the cream in a small bowl and whisk slowly into the skillet. Cook, stirring, until thickened, 5 to 7 minutes. Pour the sauce over the chicken and serve warm.

Lemon Turkey Stir-Fry

Serves 4 to 6

2 teaspoons cornstarch

2 teaspoons Worcestershire sauce

1 teaspoon soy sauce

2 teaspoons grated lemon zest

1 teaspoon chicken bouillon dissolved in ⅔ cup boiling water

2 tablespoons olive oil

1 pound cubed turkey breast

½ cup sliced green onions

½ cup sliced celery

½ cup chopped red bell pepper

1 (8-ounce) can water chestnuts, drained

1 (6-ounce) package frozen peas, thawed

2 tablespoons lemon juice

¼ teaspoon black pepper

Cooked rice, for serving (optional)

In a small bowl, combine the cornstarch, Worcestershire sauce, soy sauce, and lemon zest and mix until smooth. Stir the dissolved bouillon into the cornstarch mixture. Set aside.

Heat the olive oil in a large nonstick skillet over medium heat and stir-fry the turkey until no longer pink, about 10 minutes; remove and keep warm. In the same pan, stir-fry the onions, celery, and red pepper in the remaining oil until crisp-tender, 7 to 10 minutes. Return the turkey to the pan.

Stir the bouillon mixture and pour it over the turkey mixture. Bring to a boil, then cook and stir for 2 minutes, or until thickened. Add the water chestnuts and peas and cook until heated through. Stir in the lemon juice and pepper. Serve over rice, if desired.

When you're camping, you'd better have some alcohol in your possession or people will not want to stay after dinner. As a bonus, you can use it for marinades.

Drunk'n Flank Steak

Serves 4 to 6

1 (2- to 2½-pound) flank steak

2 cups bourbon (we prefer Jack Daniels)

¼ cup soy sauce

3 tablespoons lime juice

2 tablespoons crushed red pepper flakes

3 tablespoons chopped garlic

½ cup chopped fresh ginger

Salt and black pepper

Throw the flank steak, bourbon, soy sauce, lime juice, red pepper flakes, garlic, ginger, and salt and pepper in a 1-gallon resealable plastic bag. Seal the bag tightly, and squeeze to mix. Let this marinate for 20 hours but no longer, because the flavor will become bitter. Any less and the steak won't absorb the bourbon flavor. Grill the meat on medium-high heat for 15 minutes, or until medium, with little pink in the middle. You may want to flip the steak with tongs every 5 minutes. Cut into the meat to make sure it's medium to medium rare.

Steak Milanese

Serves 4 to 6

2 eggs

⅓ cup 2% milk

1 to 2 cups Italian seasoned bread crumbs

4 to 6 USDA choice beef loin New York strip steaks, pounded thin

2 tablespoons olive oil

1 teaspoon garlic powder

1 tablespoon chopped shallot

1 (12-ounce) can tomato sauce

2 cups shredded mozzarella cheese, more if you prefer

In a small bowl, beat together your eggs and milk to make an egg wash. Lay out your bread crumbs on a plate or flat surface. Take your steaks and dip them into your egg wash, then dredge them in your bread crumbs until the surfaces are well coated.

Heat the olive oil and garlic powder in a medium sauté pan over medium heat, then place your breaded steaks in the pan and sear until nice and browned, about 7 minutes. Do not cook all the way through because you want to finish it in the Dutch oven.

Place the seared steaks in your Dutch oven insert and cover them with tomato sauce and mozzarella cheese. Place the insert in your Dutch oven, cover it, and put about 12 coals around the top edge and 6 coals around the outside of the bottom (not underneath). Cook for about 30 minutes, or until the steak is cooked to your liking. We like ours medium to medium rare, but there are people who like their steaks cooked well. We hate those people because they are butchering the essence of a steak—the delicious juices that pour out when you bite into it!

People will go crazy for this recipe, especially if you serve it with the Red Wine Mushroom Sauce on page 179.

Camp Roast

Serves 6 to 8

¼ cup olive oil

¼ cup chopped garlic

Salt and black pepper

1 (2½- to 3-pound) beef pot roast

1 cup chopped white onions

½ cup chopped carrots

1 cup chopped celery

2 whole russet potatoes (skin on), chopped

1 cup water

2 (14-ounce) cans condensed French onion soup

Heat the olive oil, garlic, and salt and pepper in a large sauté pan over high heat. When the oil is hot, sear the pot roast on each side, about 10 minutes per side.

Place the onions, carrots, celery, and potatoes in a Dutch oven insert, then take the seared pot roast and place it on top. Add the water and soup, and salt and pepper to your liking. Place the insert in your Dutch oven, cover it, and put 16 coals on top and 10 coals around the outside of the bottom (not underneath). Cook for 2 to 3 hours, or until the meat falls apart when you try to lift it. Check on this every 30 minutes. You may have to go through a new batch of coals (when the older coals have burned out) for this recipe because it takes a long time for the roast to cook and you want to make sure you don't overcook or undercook the meat.

Ultimate Camp Cooking's Meaty Meat Loaf

Serves 4 to 6

1 (10.75-ounce) can condensed tomato soup

1½ pounds ground beef

1 (2.8-ounce) can French fried onions

1 large egg, beaten

1 tablespoon Worcestershire sauce

½ cup seeded and chopped green bell pepper

¼ cup Italian seasoned bread crumbs

Salt and black pepper

6 small potatoes, chopped small

Thoroughly mix together ½ cup of the soup with the beef, ½ can of the French fried onions, the egg, Worcestershire sauce, green pepper, bread crumbs, and salt and pepper in a large bowl. Place the mixture in your Dutch oven insert and press it into a loaflike state. Spoon the remaining soup over the meat loaf and arrange the potatoes around it.

Cover the Dutch oven and put 16 coals on the top and 8 coals around the outside of the bottom (not underneath). Cook for 1 hour, or until the meat loaf is cooked through. Sprinkle the remaining onions over the meat loaf and bake for 3 minutes, or until the onions are golden.

Beef Stroganoff

Serves 4 to 6

2 to 2½ pounds steak tips or choice sirloin, cubed

3 tablespoons dried thyme

2 tablespoons dry mustard

3 tablespoons all-purpose flour

½ cup Worcestershire sauce

Salt and black pepper

2 tablespoons olive oil

10 white button mushrooms, quartered

2 whole green bell peppers, seeded and chopped

1 large white onion, chopped

1 (8-ounce) package cream cheese

1 (12-ounce) bag egg noodles

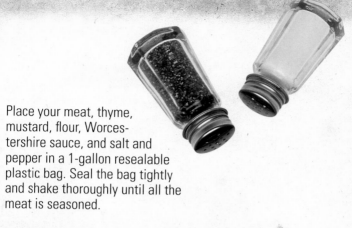

Place your meat, thyme, mustard, flour, Worcestershire sauce, and salt and pepper in a 1-gallon resealable plastic bag. Seal the bag tightly and shake thoroughly until all the meat is seasoned.

In a large sauté pan over medium heat with the olive oil, cook your seasoned meat until it begins to brown, about 7 minutes. When the meat is browned, add the vegetables and cook until the vegetables are tender and the flavors are combined. When everything has come together nicely, add your cream cheese and let that melt, cutting it up and stirring often as it cooks.

Fill a large pot with lightly salted water and bring it to a boil over medium-high heat. Once the water is boiling, stir in the egg noodles and return to a boil. Cook the noodles, uncovered, until al dente, about 11 minutes. Drain and set aside. Add the noodles to the meat mixture in the sauté pan and mix well. You can serve immediately or let this sit on a low flame until ready to serve.

Mike's Childhood Memories of Cooking

Since I was a child my fondest memories have always been waking up to the smells of freshly cooked food. For me it was burning food, but that's because my parents were as skilled at cooking as they were at parenting, which explains how I ended up a stand-up comedian instead of a respectable member of society. Just to give you an idea of names they would give their meals, my dad created his famous "garbage omelet." He called it the garbage omelet because he would put everything left in the fridge into it regardless of whether it would be appetizing in an omelet. It was called the garbage omelet because that's where it always ended up—in the garbage. Another old joke was that I used to give my dog the food because of how bad my parents' cooking was and then the dog would push the food away and say to itself, "Hell, no, I'll have myself for dinner!" My sister and I did that with a lot of meals our parents served us.

My mother would borrow recipes from her bingo friends and after a long day she would come home and experiment on us. She would make a half decent meal and we would make the mistake of letting her know that it was edible. Consequently she would get so excited about the half compliment that she would go on a cooking marathon and make this recipe for five days in a row. She would even make a meal far ahead of time with no intention of serving any of it immediately—just freezing it for later. That's never good for a meal. It was like she was trying to stock up months of meals. Now meat loaf once in a while I can tolerate; however, meat clump prepared in December but not intended to be eaten until June was not what I wanted as a growing child.

My dad, on the other hand, knew how bad he was at cooking and only cooked when it was an emergency or if we had misbehaved and wanted to torture us. My dad had two ways of driving us crazy as children: He would either throw water balloons at us while we were sitting around the house or he would cook us a meal when we were starving. Both were effective ways to drive us out of our minds, wanting to run away and live in the woods by our house.

My mother was so insecure about her cooking that she would be a nervous wreck the day before she was preparing a meal for a large group of people. She would scream and yell at both my sister and me for anything we did that broke her concentration in the preparation of her meal. My favorite pastime was to torture my parents twice as much as they tortured me. This was an everyday job, as we used to bust each other all the time. Now I would purposely ask her about the menu, which would throw a wrench in the system because anytime she would tell me an item, I would respond with a worried look and a cynical response like, "You're cooking that?!" This would set her off in such a way that she would send me to do something so insignificant just to get me out of the kitchen or make me do something so horrific it would piss me off. If I didn't do it she would sic my father on me, and he was relentless, lecturing me on being a man and a responsible adult. My dad would always give me the option of either a long speech or the belt, and I still have the belt marks to this day! That guy could talk a telemarketer into an apology.

So one year my mother decided to take on the heavy task of Thanksgiving dinner. I decided that was going to be the day I tortured her to the breaking point. We were such a close family we could do this type of thing without maliciousness. She would do the same to me, so in my opinion it was my duty. My plan was to give everyone at the dinner a cup of tea that was really an herbal diuretic. Apparently, there's a tea blend that acts in such a way that when you eat anything you have to go to the bathroom as soon as possible. I had learned this from one of my modeling friends who used it to lose weight. It would be the perfect plot to get everyone into the bathroom and make my mother believe she was responsible for making everyone sick. This was vicious, but a fine prank if I may say so myself. The plan was well thought out and strategic to the point that no one would ever know what I did and the only harm would be to my mom's ego. This was okay with me because the only long-term effect would be that my mother would never cook again, which would be good not only for the family, but for society as well. I felt like it was my civic duty to get the word out now and save a few bathrooms around the country.

My mother always liked to have a predinner where she would cook a chicken soup the night before the dinner for the immediate family. So approximately eight of us would come over the night before, sit around talking and reminiscing about stories of years past, eat, and relax. I liked this because it was kind of the calm before the storm. I didn't want to ruin this for my mother, so my plan was to serve the tea the next day before the main meal. I just pictured the scene in my head and I was in hysterics!

My mother was slaving in the kitchen as the doorbell rang. She screamed to all hell, "Can someone please get the

door!" She would shriek it like it was the twentieth time she asked, even though it was the first and the bell was rung seconds before. This was the beginning of the stress ball she would become when people came over. In years past I would get so mad at her for acting like this, but with my revenge already strategically planned I was relaxed and serene.

All the relatives came over and sat around with the same old lame stories and jokes. You remember when you were a kid listening to the same bull crap from all the same characters thinking to yourself, "When will this garbage end?" I used to get so tired of hearing yet another story about the olden days that I would slip away to catch the Red Sox scores or watch highlights of the games that afternoon. After twenty minutes of my mother screaming at me to set the table, get extra chairs from the garage, get away from the TV, and help her in the kitchen, it was time to have the long-awaited chicken soup.

In the Jewish religion, chicken soup is a delicious appetizer and it sets the tone for the entire meal. If the soup is good, then the meal should be good as well. It's Jewish medicine; it can make all the bad in your life go away. We all loved the soup and couldn't wait to sink our spoons in that thin broth filled with salty chicken taste, but remember, this was my mother cooking so my expectations were low.

My grandfather was a classic jerk. He didn't care about hurting people's feelings or about anything else, now that I think about it. He would say what was on his mind regardless of who it would crumble, which I loved because I was the same way, even as a child. This is the type of man who would take me miniature golfing just so he could beat me and talk trash the whole ride home. A real jerk, but he loved the Red Sox and he was a chronic gambler, especially on dog races. He would have stacks of dog books so high we used them as chairs when we visited him. At these family functions he would be relentless in letting everyone know how little he wanted to be there, especially for his daughter's cooking. He would always say he brought extra underwear for after the meal. We would all crack up because we felt his pain!

There were about nine of us sitting around the table ready to eat the traditional chicken soup, when all of the sudden we got a whiff of something rancid from the kitchen. It was not a very appetizing smell in the least. It smelled like roadkill. No one said anything, but we were all thinking the same thing, "What in the hell is that smell?!" My mother, who was too occupied and nervous, didn't realize she had used rotten chicken in the soup and it was stinking up the whole house. We all looked at each other, wondering who was going to be the one to say something—or would we just have to go through with it trying not to hurt her feelings? Then without skipping a beat Grandpa yells out, "Something smells like shit!" Everyone at the table just about fell off of their chairs laughing hysterically. My mother was so embarrassed, but as good family members we consoled her by telling her it would be okay, even though we were all so hungry we could've eaten the fingers off our hands at that point. You should've seen the disappointment on my mother's face. To be honest, I was a bit upset because it had ruined my plan to mess up her dinner. She had already ruined it for herself. I should've expected that; it was the only factor I didn't plan on, even though it was actually the most likely scenario. Sometimes I think I'm too smart for my own good, though. I'm kind of happy now that she ruined her own meal, because if I had done it and seen the disappointment on her face, I would have had some serious guilt for a long time. We all know how guilt can ruin a Jewish man, especially when it comes from victimizing his own mother!

Pulled Pork Taco Bar

Serves 6 to 8

1 (3- to 4-pound) pork shoulder

1 (1.25-ounce) packet taco seasoning

Salt and black pepper

¼ cup olive oil

2 (12-ounce) bottles dark beer

1 head lettuce

2 large tomatoes

1 large white onion

1 bunch cilantro

On a piece of foil, take your pork shoulder and rub it with the taco seasoning and some salt and pepper. Heat the olive oil in a large skillet over high heat, then take the pork shoulder and sear it until a crispy, crunchy layer forms on the outside. Place the pork in your Dutch oven insert and add the beer. Put the insert in the Dutch oven, cover it, and put about 16 coals on top and 8 coals around the outside of the bottom (not underneath). This is going to cook for about 2 hours. Be aware that you may have to replace the coals if they burn out without the recipe being completed. Check every 30 minutes to make sure it's cooking at a nice pace.

Shred your lettuce, chop your tomatoes and onion, dice your cilantro, and set aside. When the meat has cooled for 30 minutes, place your cut vegetables next to the meat so you can build a plate to your liking.

Blue Cheese Meatballs

Serves 4 to 6

1 pound ground beef

2 large eggs

3 tablespoons Italian seasoned bread crumbs

2 tablespoons garlic seasoning blend

2 tablespoons dried oregano

2 tablespoons dried sweet basil

2 teaspoons Italian seasoning

1 (3.5-ounce) container
blue cheese crumbles

2 tablespoons olive oil

3 tablespoons chopped garlic

Salt and black pepper

Place the beef, eggs, bread crumbs, garlic blend, oregano, basil, and Italian seasoning in a large bowl and mix well with your hands or a wooden spoon. Grab a nice handful of meat, roll it in a ball, and slam it into your hands until the meat becomes compacted and flat and makes a patty, almost like a burger. Use your fingers to make a cup in the middle for the blue cheese crumbles. Sprinkle a few chunks of blue cheese in this space, fold the meat over, and press the edges together. Gently squeeze the meat together and roll it into a ball in your hands so it becomes compacted and ready to sear.

Heat the olive oil and garlic in a medium or large pan over medium heat. Place your meatballs into the pan and cook, turning every so often, until the outsides are seared, about 7 minutes. Salt and pepper to your liking. Put the seared meatballs into your Dutch oven insert, put the insert into the Dutch oven, cover it, and put 12 coals around the top edge and 6 coals around the outside of the bottom (not underneath). Cook for 30 to 40 minutes, or until the blue cheese has melted in the meat.

Put the meatballs over some pasta with some Pink Sauce (page 175) and you will be the toast of the town!

Mexican Lasagna

Serves 4 to 6

2 (10.75-ounce) cans condensed cream of mushroom soup

1 (19-ounce) can enchilada sauce

1 pound ground beef

2 tablespoons chopped garlic

Salt and black pepper

8 flour tortillas

½ cup shredded cheddar cheese

8 hard corn tortilla shells

1 (10.75-ounce) can nacho cheese sauce

1 (14-ounce) can refried beans

In a small saucepan over medium heat, combine your soup and your enchilada sauce and let them cook together, making a creamy enchilada sauce. Keep warm over low heat.

In a medium sauté pan over medium heat, cook up your ground beef with the garlic and salt and pepper. Make sure to separate the meat well so there are no large chunks.

Put some creamy enchilada sauce on the bottom of your Dutch oven insert. Place a flour tortilla over the sauce. Add a layer of the cooked ground beef. Put some shredded cheddar cheese over that, then spread some more creamy enchilada sauce on top. Place some hard corn tortilla shells over the recipe, then add a layer of nacho cheese sauce, another layer of enchilada sauce, and the can of refried beans. Throw the rest of the ground beef over that and add another layer of cheddar cheese on top, then place the hard corn tortilla shells on top of that. Continue to do this until all the tortillas, meat, cheese, and sauce are used up or the insert is three quarters full.

Place the insert into the Dutch oven, cover it, and put about 14 coals on top and 8 coals around the outside of the bottom (not underneath). Let this cook for at least 2 hours, or until you see fit to serve.

This dish is best served with Pico de Gallo (page 134) and/or Guacamole (page 135).

Camp Fried Rice

Serves 4 to 6

Sauce

2 tablespoons unsalted butter

3 cloves garlic, chopped

½ cup soy sauce

1 cup vanilla yogurt

Rice Mixture

2 tablespoons sesame oil

2 tablespoons olive oil

2 white onions, chopped

3 carrots, chopped

3 cups chopped precooked pork

2 cups cooked white rice

2 large eggs

1 cup chopped green onions

To make your sauce, melt the butter in a small saucepan over medium heat. Add the garlic and cook until tender, about 1 minute. Slowly stir in the soy sauce and yogurt and cook until heated through. Keep the sauce warm over low heat while you make the rice mixture.

Heat the sesame oil and olive oil in a big skillet or griddle over medium heat and sauté the onions and carrots for 10 minutes. Add the pork and cook, stirring, for 5 more minutes. Add the cooked rice and stir, then add the eggs and stir constantly to scramble them in. Make sure the eggs are completely cooked, then add the sauce and cook on medium heat for 5 minutes, stirring constantly. Add the green onions and stir. Now you're ready to serve a large group of people!

Marinated Grilled Pork Tenderloin

Serves 4 to 6

1 (1½- to 2-pound) pork tenderloin

2 tablespoons chopped fresh rosemary

2 tablespoons chopped fresh thyme

2½ tablespoons chopped garlic

⅓ cup olive oil

¼ cup lemon juice

Salt and black pepper

This recipe is one we've been doing live for a few years and it's the one that gets the biggest response because of its flavor.

In a 1-gallon resealable plastic bag or large container with a lid, lay your pork tenderloin down flat. Add the rest of your ingredients, mixing well. Seal the bag or container, and let it marinate for at least 8 hours in a cooler or refrigerator. We feel it's best when the pork lies in the marinade for 20 hours if you have the patience and the willpower.

We highly recommend you cook this on a medium-high direct flame for 15 to 20 minutes on both sides. You can check the meat to see if it's cooked by pressing it with your fingers. If it is still tender it needs more time, but if it is firm to the touch, take it off and cut into the middle. It's okay if there's a little pink. Meat has a tendency to cook itself briefly after taken off a grill.

This is best served with Brown Sugar Sauce (page 180). Once you cut the pork into slices and pour some sweet brown sugar sauce over it, you've got an instant hit!

Italian Biscuit Balls

Serves 4 to 6

1 (16.3-ounce) can biscuits

¼ cup grated Parmesan cheese

2 tablespoons dried sweet basil

2 tablespoons Italian seasoning

1 (14-ounce) can tomato sauce

1 pound Italian sausage

1 (3-ounce) package pepperoni slices

1½ cups shredded mozzarella cheese

This is a great recipe either as an appetizer or a quick meal in the outdoors. You can use different meats, or if you're a vegetable lover, you can substitute your favorite vegetables for some or all of the meat.

Take your biscuits, rip them into little pieces, and roll the pieces into little balls. Put them in a 1-gallon resealable plastic bag, and add your Parmesan cheese, basil, and Italian seasoning. Seal the bag tightly and shake well until the biscuits are evenly seasoned. Dump this into your Dutch oven insert and empty an entire can of tomato sauce on top, then add your cooked Italian sausage. Arrange the pepperoni over that, then dump the mozzarella cheese on top. Put the insert into the Dutch oven, cover it, and put 14 coals on top and 7 coals around the outside of the bottom (not underneath). Cook for about 40 minutes, or until the cheese is completely melted and browned and the biscuits are raised and cooked through.

Growing Up with a Fox

As a child, I spent many summers at our cabin in McCall, Idaho. We grew up with several foxes that adopted us and spent so much time at the cabin they could have been family pets. Every spring we would show up to open the cabin and a fox would remember us and spend their lazy afternoons lakeside with us. Of course the occasional treat my father tossed out on the grass made them very happy.

When I started camping in the state park in Mc-Call a few miles from our old cabin, I wasn't surprised to see my furry friends paying a visit to my trailer. Okay, maybe it wasn't the same foxes, but word must have spread about my habit of feeding wild animals. It seems that no matter where we are a fox will recognize my whistle and approach without hesitation. To me, that is normal and one of the things I look forward to every year camping. My wife calls me the "Fox Whisperer."

One year when Mike and I were shooting our second *Ultimate Camp Cooking* DVD, we were setting up the kitchen at dusk after arriving at the state park. All of a sudden Mike jumped into the trailer doorway, pointed behind me, and said, "Be careful, dude, there is something behind you!" I turned around fast enough to startle the fox and he dashed off into the bushes. Shocked, Mike said, "Dude, that thing was right behind you!" I told him that "thing" was my pet fox and he always shows up when I'm camping. I even named him "Buddy" and he comes when I call his name. Of course, the state park rangers wouldn't be too happy with this story.

Anyway, Mike (Mr. L.A. boy) didn't believe me and said, "Yeah, right." So I got down on my knees and whistled, calling to Buddy. Within seconds the fox came out of the bushes and sat right in front of me while Mike stood in the doorway of the trailer. Mike said, "No way, dude, be careful." The fox greeted me and left after a few minutes, but I continued to laugh at the Boston-born, L.A. city boy.

—**Pat**

Beer Brats

Serves 4 to 6

1 (16-ounce) 6-pack bratwurst

2 (12-ounce) cans dark beer

1 white onion, chopped

2 tablespoons diced fresh rosemary

Lay your brats in the bottom of a large saucepan or stockpot, pour your beer over them, add the onion and rosemary, and cook over medium-high heat for about 25 minutes, or until firm. Cut the brats open to make sure they're cooked through.

Case Pasta

Serves 4 to 6

3 cups bow tie pasta

1 pound turkey sausage

2 cloves garlic, minced

2 tablespoons unsalted butter

1 (14-ounce) can chicken broth, more as needed

½ pound broccoli, chopped

8 ounces mascarpone cheese, shredded

6 ounces Parmesan cheese, shredded

1 tablespoon crushed red pepper flakes

Fill a large pot with lightly salted water and bring it to a boil over medium-high heat. Once the water is boiling, stir in the bow tie pasta and return to a boil. Cook the pasta, uncovered, until al dente, about 11 minutes. Drain and set aside.

Cook the sausage in a large sauté pan over high heat until cooked through, about 10 minutes. Add the garlic and sauté for 3 minutes. Add the butter and enough broth to cover the sausage, bring to a boil over medium-high heat, then add the broccoli and cook for 5 minutes. Reduce the heat to medium, add the cheeses, and stir until melted. Place the cooked pasta in a big bowl, add the sauce mixture, sprinkle with red pepper flakes, and serve.

Italian Spiral Pasta

Serves 4 to 6

2 tablespoons olive oil

2 pounds spicy Italian sausage

12 ounces cherry tomatoes, seeded and cut into small pieces

2 red bell peppers, seeded and chopped

1 green bell pepper, seeded and chopped

½ white onion, chopped

Salt and black pepper

1 pound spiral pasta

1 (3-ounce) package prosciutto

Heat the olive oil in a large sauté pan over medium heat and cook the sausage until almost fully cooked, about 7 minutes or until al dente. Add the tomatoes, peppers, onion, and salt and pepper to your liking. Let this cook together for a few minutes until the sausage is fully cooked and the vegetables are tender.

Fill a large pot with lightly salted water and bring to a boil over medium-high heat. Once the water is boiling, stir in the pasta and return to a boil. Cook the pasta, uncovered, until al dente, about 11 minutes. Drain it, add to the meat and vegetable mixture, and stir well. Let this sit for 30 minutes before serving to ensure maximum flavor.

Cedar Plank Salmon

Serves 4 to 6

1 (1½- to 2-pound) salmon fillet, boned

1 (1½-foot-long) cedar plank board, soaked for 12 hours

1 cup mayonnaise

2 tablespoons lemon juice

2 tablespoons chopped fresh dill

Lemon pepper, for seasoning

Salt and black pepper

Lay your salmon fillet across the cedar plank board.

In a medium-sized bowl, stir together the mayonnaise, lemon juice, dill, and a few shakes of lemon pepper. Salt and pepper to your liking. With a basting brush, apply a thick coat of lemon pepper mayonnaise across the top of the salmon fillet. Make sure to cover the entire surface so all the flavor cooks into the salmon.

This salmon is cooked over indirect heat. Turn the two outside burners on a three-burner grill to high, leaving the middle burner off. Lay the seasoned salmon in the middle where there is no direct heat. The heat from the two outside burners with create a convection effect, which in turn will cook the salmon more slowly but will help maintain the juices.

Let cook for about 1 hour, but check frequently as each grill cooks at different speeds and temperatures. Once the lemon pepper mayonnaise browns and the fish reaches the 160°F mark on a meat thermometer, the dish is done and ready to serve.

Dill Salmon

Serves 4 to 6

2 tablespoons olive oil

Salt and black pepper

1 (1½- to 2-pound) salmon fillet

1 tablespoon lemon juice

½ white onion, chopped

2 tablespoons chopped garlic

1 tablespoon chopped fresh basil

3 tablespoons chopped fresh dill

1 large lemon, sliced

This recipe is so easy to make in an aluminum foil wrap—and cleanup is easy! This is a great dish for women because it's healthy and delicious. They see this fish and want to run away with it and share it with nobody!

Take a sheet of foil and pour 1 tablespoon of olive oil on it. Sprinkle lightly with salt and pepper. Lay your salmon fillet on the oil, then pour the other tablespoon of olive oil on the surface and sprinkle lightly with salt and pepper. Squeeze some lemon juice on top. Throw your onion on top of that, along with your garlic and basil. Sprinkle with the dill, then place the sliced lemon on top of everything. Place another piece of foil on top and seal the edges of the top and bottom pieces of foil.

Grill over medium-high heat for 35 minutes, or until the salmon is cooked to your liking. Some people prefer their salmon undercooked, but we like it cooked completely through.

Barbecue Teriyaki Shrimp Scampi

Serves 4 to 6

3 tablespoons unsalted butter

2 tablespoon chopped garlic

1 pound (26 to 30 count) medium shrimp, shelled

½ cup barbecue sauce (we prefer KC Masterpiece)

⅓ cup teriyaki marinade

Salt and black pepper

This recipe is the one that people go crazy for because of the taste of the sauce created by the barbecue and teriyaki marinade. You can serve it as an appetizer or lay it over some rice or pasta.

Place an aluminum pan on your griddle over medium-high heat. Add the butter and garlic and cook for a few minutes, or until the butter is completely melted. Add the shrimp, barbecue sauce, and teriyaki marinade. Salt and pepper the whole thing and let it cook for about 15 to 20 minutes. Make sure to turn your shrimp to ensure that each side is cooked perfectly.

POTTERY BARN IN MY TRAILER

Within five minutes of purchasing a new trailer at an RV show, my wife's mind was already whirling as she began to formulate decorating ideas. She knew what needed to be done to make it a real camp trailer. Before I could buy a good pair of leather gloves and a man-sized ax, she was logged online and shopping the Pottery Barn Web site. She ordered a comforter in a color and pattern that would scale back my masculinity. She added throw pillows, matching bath towels, and a bathroom mat. The assortment of candles that followed left no room for my dignity.

With the high-thread-count sheets and duvet cover that matches the pots and pans in the cupboards, my manhood was in jeopardy. I was sure that in the future squirrels would peek inside our windows and make fun of me. Bears would point and giggle! It's really hard to defend myself to other campers while wearing a white spa robe and slippers with a hot cup of tea in one hand and a loofah in the other.

—Pat

Vegetarian

Grilled Vegetable Sandwich

Serves 4 to 6

Lemon Pepper Mayonnaise

¼ cup mayonnaise

2 tablespoons lemon juice

1 tablespoon lemon pepper seasoning

Salt and black pepper

1 eggplant, cut into ⅛-inch-thick slices

3 zucchini, cut into ⅛-inch-thick slices

2 yellow squash, cut into ⅛-inch-thick slices

1 green bell pepper sliced ⅛ inch thick

1 red bell pepper, sliced ⅛ inch thick

1 white onion, halved

8 white button mushrooms, halved

⅓ cup olive oil

1 loaf jalapeño cheese bread or focaccia

This is a great recipe if you are not a meat eater or you want something light, hearty, and delicious.

In a small bowl, combine the mayo, lemon juice, lemon pepper, and salt and pepper and mix gently for a minute. Set aside.

Put all the vegetables, the oil, and some salt and pepper in a 1-gallon resealable plastic bag. Seal the bag tightly and shake well to coat everything with the oil and seasoning.

Grill the vegetables over a medium flame until tender. Slice your bread and grill it until it browns lightly. Spread the lemon pepper mayo across your bread slices and layer on your grilled vegetables. We suggest putting the eggplant, zucchini, and squash on the bottom and then working your way up with the mushrooms, onion, and peppers, which will be harder to stack. Put them on top and push your bread down to lock them into the sandwich. Try not to stack it too high, either, because it will be hard to close and eat.

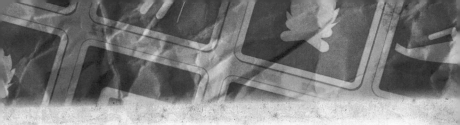

Vegetable Medley

Serves 6 to 8

8 red potatoes, quartered

1 (15-ounce) can chicken broth

12 white button mushrooms, halved

1 large white onion, chopped

3 zucchini, chopped

2 acorn squash, chopped

4 carrots, chopped

¼ cup chopped garlic

¼ cup chopped fresh sweet basil

3 tablespoons chopped fresh rosemary

¼ cup olive oil

Salt and black pepper

Place the potatoes and broth in a medium-sized pot and cook over medium-high heat for about 8 minutes, or until cooked through. Pierce one with a fork; if it goes completely through easily it's done. Make sure they're not completely cooked through as they will finish in the Dutch oven later.

Place the mushrooms, onion, zucchini, squash, carrots, garlic, basil, rosemary, olive oil, and salt and pepper in a large bowl. Stir to mix well. (You can also put the whole thing in a 1-gallon resealable plastic bag, seal it tightly, and shake it up well.)

Throw the seasoned vegetables in your Dutch oven insert, put it in the Dutch oven, cover, and put 10 coals on the top and 6 coals around the outside of the bottom (not underneath), Cook for 20 to 30 minutes, or until the vegetables are browned or cooked through.

Pasta Primavera

Serves 4 to 6

⅓ cup unsalted butter

½ cup chopped onion

½ cup seeded and chopped green bell pepper

½ cup chopped eggplant

½ cup chopped zucchini

½ cup chopped yellow squash

½ cup seeded and chopped tomato

¼ cup chopped carrot

2 tablespoons chopped garlic

Salt and black pepper

1½ cups heavy whipping cream

8 ounces angel hair pasta

¾ cup shredded Parmesan cheese

Melt the butter in a large sauté pan over medium heat. Add all the chopped vegetables and salt and pepper, and sauté until the vegetables are cooked through. Add your whipping cream and cook until it makes a thick sauce, about 10 minutes. You can check it with a spoon. If you dip your spoon into the sauce and it drips, it needs more time. If you dip your spoon and the sauce sticks to the spoon without dripping, it is ready to serve.

Fill a large pot with lightly salted water and bring it to a boil over medium-high heat. Once the water is boiling, stir in the pasta and return to a boil. Cook the pasta, uncovered, until al dente, about 11 minutes. Drain the pasta and put it in an aluminum pan. Add the vegetables and sauce to the pasta and mix it up well. Sprinkle the Parmesan cheese on top and serve it up!

Pat's Story: How It All Started

I married into a family that had a long history of spending time together in the mountains camping. They had been camping together in Idaho since the kids were barely walking. I grew up camping and backpacking, but spent most of my childhood at a mountain lakeside cottage in McCall, Idaho—you know, the rough life. Both families had the same philosophy, though: Food and drinks make for a happy weekend.

The only problem was that my wife wasn't into camping with the rest of her family. She had decided in her thirties that she preferred to check into a hotel with room service and a spa. Her idea of roughing it was continental breakfast at a Super 8. While she was working on her master's degree, her family convinced me to make trips with them to the mountains without her. I would return home smelling like a fire pit and greasy burgers, talking about how much fun we had had and how much we had eaten and drank. (Little did she know, we would also sit around the campfire and make fun of her for not joining us.) Her parents would later help feed my new addiction with camp cooking supplies for my birthday and Christmas. With each gift, my wife would call me a traitor and book a room for us at the nearest spa.

Finally, with constant pleading from me and her family, my wife gave in and said she would join the rest of us dirt-ridden camp dwellers, but she had some serious demands:

backpack (chiefly US),
daypack (US),
rucksack (chiefly Brit)

air mattress, air bed

1 We must have a toilet inside the tent. No getting up in the middle of the night and peeing in the woods.

2 We must have a blow-up mattress situated up off the ground, with high-thread-count sheets.

3 We must have coffee in bed in the morning before getting up. (Guess whose job it was to make the coffee?)

4 We must have a hot shower.

Not simple demands, but I wanted to share the camping experience with her enough that I pulled some strings and fulfilled her wishes. I figured out how to set up a solar shower in the woods, and after that the other three demands were not too difficult. Then I wanted to up the ante and bring gourmet foods into the mix. I would tell people it was one of wife's requirements, when in fact I was using her as an excuse to feed my demands of liking good food. That is when my new philosophy for camping came in to effect: "When you are camping you are on vacation and when you are on vacation you should eat well."

I grew up in my dad's restaurant as a kid and spent a lot time in the kitchen with the chefs, watching and learning the tricks of the trade. I was in fourth grade when I put on my first chef's hat (with extra pins because it was too big for my head). Now some might say my head is too big for a chef's hat! I was being paid $2.00 a day for my work; Sweatshop owners seem like saints compared to my dad.

I went from the kitchen of my dad's restaurant, Michael's, in Boise, Idaho, to mixing drinks behind the bar (at an illegal age) during the slower hours. Back in those days, when the mayor and police chief were your customers, no one said anything. With my cooking skills up to par and my spirit mixing skills on track, I was ready to achieve the title of "Almighty Camp Chef." Okay, that might be a little much, but I was ready to spice up these family outings, pun intended.

I would plan a menu for the entire weekend based on gourmet comfort food and lots of it. I would build an outdoor kitchen area away from everyone just to keep the grubby finger food pickers away. At home, when you are having a party, the crowd always congregates in the kitchen, and the same applies to the outdoor kitchen.

I would assemble a separate canopy with two tables for my grill, stove, oven, skillet, and a couple boxes of kitchen utensils. I also had a table with two built-in sinks and a drying rack, and a cupboard that would hang in the kitchen and hold all the spices and oils that would go unused for the most part (just like they did at home), but it sure looked good.

One day, my brother in-law, Dexter, was helping me clean up in the makeshift kitchen after a simple breakfast of Dutch Oven Benedict (page 38) with Rosemary Red Potatoes (page 144) and fresh biscuits. While I was prepping a Drunk'n Flank Steak (page 91) with bourbon, garlic, soy sauce, and crushed red pepper flakes for dinner, Dexter made a suggestion that would change the course of my life. "You need to make a DVD of these recipes. You could combine your three favorite things (cooking, camping, and comedy) and make a career of it," he said.

As a professional stand-up comedian I spent a lot of time on the road traveling from city to city, working comedy clubs and colleges. I had a couple of nights off in Houston, Texas, and was hanging out at the comedy club for open mic night. While waiting to go on stage, I was sitting in the back of the room with fellow comedians and friends. One of those comedians was Mike. We sat and chatted about the business and who we knew, and we traded numbers to network with each other. We stayed in touch, calling each other a few times over a two-year period.

I took over a comedy club in my hometown and started booking the acts, and one of the first calls I made was to Mike. I booked him to come to Boise for two weeks in the spring. One of my employees hosted a barbecue at the end of the two weeks with lots of alcohol and good food. With most of the partygoers hanging out outside, Mike and I ended up prepping all the food and putting together everyone's recipes. He told me that he used to be a chef and loved to cook, and I talked about my love for camp cooking and that I always wanted to make a DVD of camp cooking in the mountains. He owned a production company and we decided to get together and make a DVD.

Five months later, we headed to McCall, Idaho, with a shopping list, camera, and my pop-up tent trailer and produced our first DVD. History was made and campers around the world will be forever victimized by Mike and me.

An update on my wife: She loves camping, especially now that we have a trailer, but she still books great exotic trips. She can still get her massage, and I can get great recipes from the locals. Thanks to Karen's family, we are both happy and loving life!

Portabella Mushroom Steaks

Serves 4 to 6

2 tablespoons soy sauce

1 tablespoon liquid smoke

3 tablespoons white wine vinegar

1 cup balsamic vinegar

Salt and black pepper

6 to 8 portabella mushroom caps (the larger the better), stems removed

These are great on a sandwich or as an appetizer. You will be amazed by the flavor the mushroom absorbs as it grills!

Combine the soy sauce, liquid smoke, vinegars, and salt and pepper on a rimmed baking sheet.

Place the mushroom caps open-end down into the marinade. This will ensure that the mushroom absorbs as much of the marinade as possible. Marinate for 4 hours, then turn the mushrooms on their backs and marinate for another couple of hours.

Grill the mushrooms over medium-low direct heat. You don't want to cook on high because you will cook out the flavor.

ULTIMATE CAMP COOKING

SIDE DISHES

Pico de Gallo

Serves 4 to 6

⅓ cup finely diced white onion

2 tablespoons minced garlic

3 large tomatoes, seeded and diced

2 jalapeños, seeded and diced

2 tablespoon chopped fresh cilantro

2 tablespoons lemon juice

Salt and black pepper

Throw your vegetables and cilantro into a medium bowl. Add the lemon juice, then salt and pepper to your liking. Let this sit for at least an hour before serving.

Note: If you are cutting jalapeños, make sure to wear rubber gloves so the juice doesn't burn your fingers.

Guacamole

Serves 4 to 6

3 large tomatoes, seeded and finely diced

⅓ cup finely diced white onion

2 tablespoons minced garlic

2 jalapeños, seeded and finely diced (optional)

2 tablespoon diced cilantro

2 tablespoons lemon juice

Salt and black pepper

3 large ripe avocados, halved and pitted

Throw the tomatoes, onion, garlic, jalapeños (if using), and cilantro into a medium bowl. Add the lemon juice and salt and pepper to your liking. Scoop out the soft avocado flesh and use a fork or spoon to mash it into the rest of the ingredients. Let this sit for at least an hour before serving.

This is great served with some corn chips or as a side with Mexican Lasagna (page 106).

Note: If you throw the avocado pits into the guacamole, they will help oxygenate the avocados so they don't turn brown.

Blue Cheese Green Beans

Serves 4 to 6

8 strips bacon

5 ounces green beans

⅓ cup chopped white onion

3 tablespoons chopped garlic

1 (5-ounce) container Gorgonzola cheese

This recipe takes green beans, which some people might be reluctant to eat, and turns it into an unhealthy yet delicious side dish everyone will crave!

Lay a piece of aluminum foil on a table, lay 4 strips of bacon down, then add your green beans, onion on top of the beans, garlic, and another layer of bacon on top of all that. Close with another piece of foil and seal the edges. Place on a griddle or grill over medium heat or in the fire, and cook for about 30 minutes. Open up the foil, check and make sure the bacon has cooked, then add the Gorgonzola cheese, close it again, and cook for another 10 minutes, until the cheese is melted.

New Trailer Owners or First-Time Campers, Listen Up!

You and your significant other have just purchased your first trailer, tent trailer, or tent and are ready to head out for your first camping trip. You're excited and can't wait to get to your campsite to set up and spend the night in your wonderful new purchase.

Take these steps and you should make it back without a divorce:

1. Before you leave, make a checklist of everything you will need, from flashlights, to bug spray, sunscreen, and so forth.

2. Assign each person a task before you arrive and make sure you already know how to set up that new tent or trailer. Stick to those tasks until the camp set-up is complete.

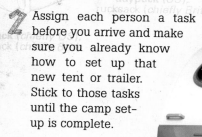

3 If you have small children, figure out ahead of time how you're going to keep them busy while you set up. (And what the hell were you thinking anyway?)

4 Make sure the cooler is easily accessible to get the cold beer out during setup to take the edge off.

If you have a new trailer, my best suggestion ever is to hook up and go to a parking lot with your partner and practice unhooking and setting up. Know ahead of time what hand signals you want to use and what they mean. Learn where the sight line is in the rearview and side mirrors. Make sure the outside guide knows how to stay in the mirror range. Know what swear words are okay and not okay. This could save you a lot of alimony. There is nothing more fun than watching new campers yelling and screaming obscenities at each other while on vacation, especially as you and your significant other are peacefully toasting to a successful setup!

—Pat

backpack (*chiefly US*),
daypack (*US*),
rucksack (*chiefly Brit*)

air mattress, air bed

Asian Asparagus

Serves 4 to 6

1 bunch asparagus, blunt ends trimmed

4 cloves garlic, chopped

¼ cup soy sauce

2 tablespoons sesame oil

2 tablespoons sesame seeds

Place all the ingredients in a 1-gallon resealable plastic bag. Seal the bag tightly, shake vigorously, and let marinate for 12 to 24 hours. Grill the asparagus for 8 to 10 minutes on the grill over direct heat until tender.

Candied Asparagus

Serves 4 to 6

Sea salt

1 tablespoon olive oil

1 bunch asparagus, blunt ends trimmed

2 tablespoons unsalted butter

¼ cup packed brown sugar

1 (3.5-ounce) bag sliced almonds, toasted

Fill a large pot with water, add the sea salt and olive oil, and bring to a boil over high heat. Cook the asparagus until tender, about 7 minutes. Strain it out and place in an ice bath. This will help maintain the chlorophyll in the asparagus and keep it green and crisp.

Melt the butter in a medium sauté pan over low heat, then add the asparagus, brown sugar, and toasted almonds. Let them cook for about 5 minutes, or until the brown sugar is bubbling in the butter. This will make a sweet sauce that will coat the asparagus completely, making what could be a very bland vegetable into a sweet candylike delight!

Pancetta-Stuffed Mushrooms

Serves 8 to 10

15 to 20 large white button mushrooms

8 ounces pancetta

1 cup grated fresh Parmesan cheese

1 tablespoon chopped garlic

2 tablespoons olive oil

Remove the stems from your mushrooms. Save 6 of them, chop them up, and set them aside. Place the mushroom caps dome-up on your grill over direct heat for 10 minutes. Chill the mushrooms, then drain any excess water from them.

Place the pancetta in a sauté pan over medium heat and cook until browned and crispy, up to 7 minutes.

In a 1-gallon resealable plastic bag, combine the chopped mushroom stems, cheese, garlic, pancetta, and olive oil. Seal the bag tightly and shake to mix well. Stuff the mixture into the mushroom caps. Place the mushrooms in a Dutch oven insert, placing 10 coals on top and 5 coals around the outside of the bottom (not underneath), and let them cook for about 20 minutes, or until the Parmesan cheese melts. Serve immediately and stay close because they will be gone in minutes.

Dad's Potatoes

Serves 6 to 8

3 tablespoons unsalted butter, at room temperature

Salt and black pepper, for seasoning

Celery salt, for seasoning

Garlic powder, for seasoning

1 pound seasoned Tater Tots

½ cup chopped white onion

½ cup seeded and chopped green bell pepper

½ cup sliced white button mushrooms

½ cup chopped zucchini

Lay 2 feet of aluminum foil on a table and rub some butter along the middle. Add salt and pepper, celery salt, and garlic powder. Don't overseason, because the Tater Tots are preseasoned. Put the Tater Tots across the butter, then add the chopped vegetables.

Fold up the sides of the foil, making a canoe, then fold up the ends to ensure that none of the mixture falls out. Now take another piece of foil, wrap it around the air pocket, and roll like a newspaper.

Cook for 15 to 20 minutes on both sides over medium-high heat either on a griddle or grill, or in a fire pit. It's done when all the vegetables are cooked through.

The great thing about this recipe is you can either cook it immediately or throw it in your fridge or cooler and cook it later. This is a good side dish while you're camping. Because of the foil wrap there is absolutely no cleanup. Everyone likes that.

Rosemary Red Potatoes

Serves 6

¼ cup olive oil

3 tablespoons chopped garlic

Salt and black pepper

20 red potatoes, skin on, cut in ¼-inch slices

3 tablespoons diced fresh rosemary

3 tablespoons diced fresh thyme

Heat the olive oil, garlic, and salt and pepper in a large skillet or griddle over medium-low heat. Let that sizzle until the garlic is dancing like a drunk kid at a prom, then add the sliced potatoes, rosemary, and thyme. The herbs will adhere to the potatoes and really flavor up this recipe. Cook for about 25 minutes. We like our potatoes crispy, which will take more time and patience. If you prefer them a little less cooked, keep an eye on them and you will know when it's time to chow down!

Potato Gratin

Serves 4 to 6

4 tablespoons (½ stick) unsalted butter

3 tablespoons chopped garlic

2 tablespoons chopped shallots

Salt and black pepper

1½ to 2 cups heavy whipping cream

8 to 10 large Yukon Gold potatoes, sliced ⅛ inch thick and soaked in water for 20 minutes to get rid of the starch

1 cup grated Parmesan cheese

This is one of our favorite recipes—a crowd pleaser!

Melt the butter in a large sauté pan over medium heat. Add the garlic, shallots, and salt and pepper and cook until the garlic is dancing. Then add your cream and heat until the cream begins to thicken up. A great way to tell if the cream is thickening is to take a spoon and dip it into the cream. If it sticks without any cream dripping off the spoon it's thickening perfectly.

Once the cream is thick like a sauce, add your potatoes and cook for about 15 minutes, or until the potatoes are almost completely cooked through. This could take different amounts of time depending on your elevation. Once the potatoes are cooked through, dump them into your Dutch oven insert and spread them evenly, almost like a pie, then cover the mixture with Parmesan cheese. Cover the Dutch oven and put 12 coals on top and 6 coals around the outside of the bottom (not underneath). Cook for about 45 minutes, or until the Parmesan cheese is completely melted. Take the insert out and let the potatoes cool a little before serving.

Bacon Mac and White Cheese

Serves 6 to 8

¼ cup plus 1 tablespoon
grated Parmesan cheese

1 pound short penne pasta

1 pound thick sliced bacon, minced

4 tablespoons (½ stick) unsalted butter

1 small white onion, chopped

⅓ cup all-purpose flour

4 cups 2% milk

1 teaspoon dried ground thyme

Salt and black pepper

3½ cups shredded sharp
white cheddar cheese

Grease your Dutch oven insert and sprinkle about 1 tablespoon of the Parmesan cheese around the inside of the dish.

Fill a large pot with lightly salted water and bring it to a boil over medium-high heat. Once the water is boiling, stir in the penne and return to a boil. Cook the penne, uncovered, until al dente, about 11 minutes. Drain and set aside.

Place the bacon pieces into a large, deep skillet and cook over medium-high heat, stirring occasionally, until evenly browned, about 10 minutes. Drain the bacon on a paper towel–lined plate. Reserve ¼ cup of the bacon drippings. Set the bacon pieces aside.

Melt the butter and bacon drippings together in a large saucepan over medium heat. Add the onion and cook and stir until translucent, about 5 minutes. Whisk in the flour, stirring frequently, until the mixture forms a smooth paste. Whisk in the milk a little at a time and bring the mixture to a simmer, whisking constantly until thickened. Stir in the thyme and salt and pepper, then whisk in the remaining ¼ cup of Parmesan and 3 cups of cheddar cheese, stirring constantly until the cheese has melted and the sauce is smooth and thick.

Stir the cooked penne pasta into the cheese sauce, then gently mix in the cooked bacon. Spread the mixture into the prepared baking dish and sprinkle the remaining ½ cup of cheddar cheese over the top. Cover the dish with foil.

Place this in your Dutch oven, cover it, and put 10 coals on top and 6 coals around the outside of the bottom (not underneath). Cook for about 25 minutes, or until the top layer has browned, then remove the bottom coals and place them on top for about 5 more minutes. This will act like a broiler and broil the dish until the cheese topping is more browned and crisp.

Dirty Rice

Serves 4 to 6

4 tablespoons olive oil

1 pound ground beef

Salt and black pepper

2 sprigs rosemary, chopped

2 tablespoons chopped fresh thyme

1 tablespoon chopped fresh basil

2 tablespoons chopped garlic

3 tablespoons unsalted butter

1 large green bell pepper, seeded and chopped

8 white button mushrooms, sliced

½ large white onion, chopped

2 large tomatoes, chopped

1 (8-ounce) box seasoned rice
(we prefer Zatarain's)

Heat 2 tablespoons of olive oil in a large sauté pan over medium heat. Place the ground beef in the pan and fry it up, adding the salt and pepper, rosemary, thyme, basil, and garlic as the meat cooks.

Melt the butter in a medium sauté pan over medium heat. Add the green pepper, mushrooms, and onion and cook until they are almost transparent, about 7 minutes. Add the tomatoes last because they cook the fastest and you want it all to be done at the same time and consistency. Salt and pepper to your liking. Add the vegetable mixture to the meat mixture and let them sit in each other's juices while you prepare the rice.

In a large saucepan, bring 1 cup of water and the remaining 2 table-spoons of olive oil and salt to a boil over medium heat. Add the rice mixture and cook for about 8 minutes, or until partially cooked. The water will not be entirely absorbed and the rice will not be plump. You want the rice to start to absorb the water before you continue with the recipe. When the rice has partially cooked, add the meat and vegetable mixture to it. Let them finish cooking together, stirring constantly, for about 15 minutes. You may want to let the rice sit for a few minutes, unless there is someone at your table you'd like to see burn the top of their mouth! ;)

When Is the Best Time to Buy a New Trailer?

It was January in Boise, Idaho, and my wife, Karen, and I were going stir crazy to go camping, so we went to the Idaho RV show at the fairgrounds instead. We did not go to buy anything, only to look at trailers. Let me be clear on this, we were just looking and not buying. Or so I thought.

The last time we had gone to the show, we had bought our pop-up tent trailer, thanks to my wife, aka "Impulsive Nancy." So I knew what I was up against already. We do not have a safe word, and there is no way to reason with her when her eyes start to dilate and the words "We'll take it!" come out of her mouth.

We walked up to the gate and paid the entry fee. I went to put my wallet back in my pocket when I noticed my wife was already gone. I scanned the area on my tippytoes and looked at the sea of trailers. I saw her walking up the steps of the first trailer of the thousands on display. I quickly gave my ticket to the gate person and made my way over to the trailer, where I could hear her inside talking with the salesman. She said, "Does this one come in another color or with a different border of wallpaper?"

Before I could stop her she said, "We'll take it," and followed that with, "You can take the flat-screen TV, microwave oven, and surround sound system out, though. We won't be using those." I was speechless.

The salesman answered, "Those are standard and come with it already."

Again she said, "We'll still take it!" I quickly took her aside and explained that we were at an RV and trailer show, there were hundreds of other trailers to see, and her negotiating skills sucked! I told her "We'll take it" is what you say after you've talked the price down, not what you say when the salesman shows you the price sign.

The rest of the talk went well. We signed the papers for the new trailer five minutes later, and then walked around and looked at other units. If you ever wanted to buy a new trailer or were looking to upgrade, an RV and trailer show is the way to go. You will save thousands of dollars, and if you're lucky you'll get to compare units before purchasing one!

—Pat

Gorgonzola Pasta Salad

Serves 6 to 8

1 (9-ounce) bag tricolor spiral pasta (about 3 cups)

1 (5-ounce) container Gorgonzola cheese (see Note)

1 cup chopped cooked crispy bacon

3 tablespoons chopped fresh basil

1 cup seeded and chopped cherry tomatoes

⅓ cup olive oil

⅓ cup red wine vinegar

2 tablespoons lemon juice

Salt and black pepper

Italian seasoning

Fill a large pot with lightly salted water and bring to a boil over medium-high heat. Once the water is boiling, stir in the pasta and return to a boil. Cook the pasta, uncovered, until al dente, about 11 minutes. Drain the pasta, then quickly add your Gorgonzola cheese to the pot, stirring well. You want the pasta hot so that the cheese melts with the pasta. Add your bacon, basil, tomatoes, olive oil, vinegar, lemon juice, and salt and pepper and mix well. Stir in the Italian seasoning to your liking. We believe you become a chef when you no longer need measuring cups and you just add to taste to see how you like it!

Note: You can substitute feta cheese for Gorgonzola and also add olives if you like. You can also grill up some pancetta or prosciutto, crumble it, and throw that in, too. There are many different ways to make this recipe.

ULTIMATE
CAMP
COOKING

SOUPS AND
SALADS

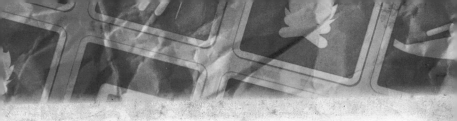

Potato Cheddar Soup

Serves 4 to 6

2 cups peeled and cubed red potatoes

4 tablespoons (½ stick) unsalted butter

1 white onion, chopped

2 tablespoons
all-purpose flour

½ teaspoon sugar

3 cups 2% milk

1½ cups shredded
cheddar cheese

2 cups chicken broth

1 cup diced ham

Salt and black pepper

Fill a large saucepan with water, add your potatoes, and bring to a boil over medium-high heat. Cook until the potatoes are fork-tender, about 15 minutes, then reserve 1 cup of the boiling water and discard the rest.

To the potatoes, add the butter, onion, flour, sugar, reserved potato water, milk, cheese, chicken broth, and ham. Mix well and cook on low heat for about 20 minutes, stirring often. Salt and pepper to your liking. The whole thing is done when all the ingredients come together and begin to thicken when stirring.

Three-Mushroom Soup

Serves 4 to 6

⅓ cup unsalted butter

2 tablespoons chopped garlic

1 tablespoon chopped shallot

2 cups chopped shiitake mushrooms

2 cups chopped button mushrooms

2 cups chopped portabella mushrooms

3 (14-ounce) cans chicken broth

Salt and black pepper

Melt your butter in a large sauté pan over medium heat. Add the garlic and shallot, and sauté until fragrant, about 5 minutes. Add all three types of mushrooms and sauté until they reduce, 7 to 10 minutes. Working in three batches, scoop out 1 cup of mushrooms and place them in a blender along with 1 cup of chicken broth. Blend on medium speed for about 15 seconds. Repeat with the remaining mushrooms and broth. Salt and pepper to your liking.

Dump the puree into your Dutch oven insert, cover it, and put 10 coals on top and 6 coals around the outside of the bottom (not underneath). Cook for about 45 minutes, or until hot and ready to serve. Flavor is very important in this recipe, so continue to add salt and pepper until its flavor pops out at you!

EVOLUTION OF A CAMPER

My wife and I went through the different phases of camping most couples go through and our desire for comfort expanded as our camping experiences did.

I started out in a four-man tent with plenty of room for me and my one-inch mat. Then my wife joined me, but she was not happy about the prospect of tent camping at her age. To try to make her more comfortable, I moved up to a ten-man condo tent that stood eight feet tall, along with a blow-up mattress, nightstand, chair, and a portable bathroom. Those things alone took almost two hours to set up and three hours to take down. Full camp setup time equaled four hours or ten beers. By the time I was done, I looked like I had just run a marathon—I was completely soaked in sweat.

After two years of walking around campgrounds, checking out campsites, and seeing others in their pop-up tent trailers, we started yearning for an even more comfortable experience. Some of our friends started buying pop-up

trailers, so we bought one, too. Finally we had a comfortable bed off of the ground, a door that locked, a built-in kitchen, and storage for our camping equipment. No more taking hours to set up our tent, cleaning it, and crawling around on our hands and knees. In time we figured out that a pop-up still takes some time to put together after unhooking, and the same goes for breaking down. We still had to make the beds and pull everything out to build our camp, and we had to use a portable bathroom in the middle of the night. Full camp setup time equaled one hour or four beers.

We were really happy with our new setup for about two or three years. Then as we strolled around the campgrounds in the evening checking out other campsites we began to notice how relaxed the travel trailer owners seemed. The trailer owners kicked back with a cool beverage and a knowing smile, watching us set up our pop-up. Consequently, the same friends who had bought a pop-up before upgraded to a travel trailer. So we bought a travel trailer, too, and setup consisted of unhooking the camper, leveling, pushing a button to extend the electric awning, hooking up the water, setting out the gravity chairs, and grabbing a cold one. Full camp setup time equaled fifteen minutes or one beer.

Two other groups who joined us followed our lead as well; I can't wait for our friends to buy a large mondo-RV with five slide-outs so we can do the same. My wife says she is happy with our current home away from home, but it will be interesting to see what evolves as we take our nightly strolls around the campgrounds.

My advice to first-time campers who want to get their feet wet is to spend two days in a closet with your wife, kids, and a wet dog with the door closed. Just make sure you have one or more cold beers with you.

—Pat

Mexican Chicken Soup

Serves 4 to 6

2 tablespoons olive oil

2 cloves garlic, minced

2 stalks celery, diced

2 cups chopped onions

2 pounds boneless skinless chicken breast, chopped

2 teaspoons ground cumin

½ teaspoon ground oregano

1 teaspoon ground coriander

2 (4.5-ounce) cans green chiles, drained

2 (15-ounce) cans cannellini beans, drained and rinsed

1 (32-ounce) container chicken broth

Chopped fresh cilantro, for serving

Shredded pepper Jack cheese, for serving

Heat the olive oil in a large soup pot over medium-high heat. Add the garlic, celery, and onions and sauté for 8 minutes, or until the vegetables are transparent Add the chicken and sauté until cooked through, about 7 minutes. Add the cumin, oregano, coriander, chiles, beans, and chicken broth to the pot and simmer for 20 minutes. Serve with chopped cilantro and shredded pepper Jack cheese on top.

Italian Soup
(Don't ask—just eat it!)

Serves 4 to 6

1 pound spicy ground sausage

1 green bell pepper, seeded and finely chopped

1 red bell pepper, seeded and finely chopped

2 tablespoons olive oil

1 yellow onion, finely chopped

½ vine cherry tomatoes, halved and seeded

1 tablespoon ground oregano

1 teaspoon cayenne pepper

1 teaspoon Cajun seasoning

1 (32-ounce) container beef broth

1 (15-ounce) can tomato sauce

1 (12-ounce) can tomato paste

2 cups cooked elbow macaroni

Combine the sausage, green and red pepper, olive oil, and onion in a large soup pot cook over high heat until the sausage is halfway done, about 8 minutes. Reduce the heat to medium, add the tomatoes, oregano, cayenne, and Cajun seasoning, mix well, and cook for 20 to 30 minutes. Stir in the beef broth, tomato sauce, and tomato paste and cook for 20 minutes more. Finally, add the cooked macaroni and cook for 5 minutes to heat through.

This is great with crusty bread and an ice-cold beer!

Pat Mac's Chili

Serves 6 to 8

2 tablespoons olive oil

2 tablespoons chopped garlic

Salt and black pepper

1 white onion, chopped

2 green bell peppers, seeded and chopped

1 cup red wine

1 pound maple sausage

1 pound ground beef

1 (1.25-ounce) packet chili seasoning

1 (12-ounce) bottle dark beer

1 (15-ounce) can tomato sauce

1 (28-ounce) can crushed tomatoes

1 (15-ounce) can kidney beans

1 (14-ounce) can chili beans

1 (14-ounce) can beef broth

1 (10-ounce) can Rotel Tomatoes & Green Chiles

1 (6-ounce) can tomato paste

1 (4.5-ounce) can green chiles

2 tablespoons liquid smoke

Heat the olive oil in a large soup pot over medium heat. Add the garlic and salt and pepper, and cook until fragrant, about 5 minutes. Add the onion and peppers and sauté until transparent, about 7 minutes. Increase the heat to high, add the wine, and cook until the wine reduces and absorbs into the vegetables, about 8 minutes. Add the sausage and ground beef and cook thoroughly, about 15 minutes, chopping them up as they cook. If you add the remaining ingredients too soon, the meat will stop cooking and it could be unsafe to eat.

Once the meat is fully cooked, add the chili seasoning and mix well so all the meat gets seasoned, about 3 minutes more cooking time. Add the dark beer and cook for 3 more minutes, making sure the dark beer gets a chance to absorb into the vegetables and meat and some of the alcohol burns off. Salt and pepper to your liking. Dump all the canned ingredients, from the tomato sauce to the chiles, into the pot, finish with the liquid smoke, and stir it all up. Simmer on low heat at least until it's all heated through but ideally for as long as you can—until you just can't wait any longer. The longer you let it simmer, the more the flavors come together. If it's been cooking for a while, you may have to let it cool a little before serving.

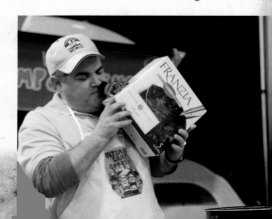

PAT TAKES HIS CHILI SERIOUSLY

The first three years Mike and I traveled with our cooking show we cooked over 500 pots of chili from a recipe I created. Then when I come home my wife and our friends would request a batch. Seriously? Don't you understand that I make this recipe in my sleep and hate it now? Don't you realize what will happen to me if I make this recipe one more time?

I never knew how to make good chili when I started out cooking, but it seemed that all good chefs had their own chili recipe to claim, so I needed one. I went online and researched all the winning chili recipes, looked at the secret ingredients that made them win, and combined them all into one chili. Crazy, huh? Yeah, crazy like a fox.

Maple sausage won one year, dark beer the next, and red wine after that. I found several other key ingredients, made a list, went to the store, and got to work figuring out how to create my masterpiece. I went to teach a cooking class that night and used this recipe. The owner of the shop didn't know how to react when I told her that I was teaching a recipe I hadn't even tried yet. She looked over my shoulder the entire time, wondering if she would have to refund the class participants' money.

Once the chili was done simmering and everyone had a taste, even I was shocked. The class never knew it was my first shot at the recipe, and no one asked for a refund. I have tweaked the recipe over time and perfected it during our live shows, but now I have a hard time eating a complete bowl myself.

During our shows I would have to chop over twenty onions and twenty green peppers at the beginning of the week to prep for it. I found the best way to chop onions without crying like a fourteen-year-old girl whose boyfriend broke up with her is to put the onions in the fridge for at least three hours before you cut them, which makes them easier to chop.

My biggest pet peeve while serving chili during or after our live show to some of the attendees is when a few would say, "No thanks, I make my own at home." Good for you, Emeril. I don't care if you make your own, the least you can do is try a different chili and have an open mind. We are always open to new suggestions from our audience! We certainly get to meet all walks of life at the live shows, and every day is a culinary adventure.

Camp Beef Stew

Serves 6 to 8

2 tablespoons olive oil

1½ to 2 pounds stew beef, cubed

2 tablespoons chopped garlic

1 (28-ounce) can diced tomatoes

2 beef bouillon cubes

2 teaspoons sugar

⅓ cup chopped carrot

½ cup chopped celery

2 large russet potatoes, skin on, chopped

1 cup chopped white onion

Salt and black pepper

Heat the olive oil in a large soup pot over medium heat and cook the meat and garlic until the meat is completely cooked through. Add the tomatoes, 4 cups of water, the beef bouillon, sugar, carrot, celery, potatoes, onion, and salt and pepper, and cook until the broth thickens, about 15 minutes. Once the broth thickens a bit, turn the heat down to low and cook for about 1 hour.

You can also put everything in a Dutch oven insert and let it cook in the Dutch oven for 1 hour and 40 minutes with 16 coals around the top edge and 8 coals around the outside of the bottom (not underneath).

This thick stew will keep people full throughout the night. Even the bears will want to rip into your kitchen for a late-night snack!

Pesto Shrimp Salad

Serves 4 to 6

⅓ cup unsalted butter

2 tablespoons chopped garlic

Salt and black pepper

1 pound (26 to 30 count) medium shrimp

¾ cup prepared pesto

1 (12-ounce) bag spring salad mix

1 (12-ounce) bag romaine hearts

1 (3-ounce) canister feta cheese crumbles (add more if you like)

⅓ cup shredded Parmesan cheese

6 white button mushrooms, sliced

8 whole cherry tomatoes

2 avocados, peeled, pitted, and sliced

1 red bell pepper, seeded and sliced

1 yellow bell pepper, seeded and sliced

1 green bell pepper, seeded and sliced

1 or 2 hard-boiled eggs, sliced (optional)

2 tablespoons balsamic vinaigrette dressing

This is an amazing dish before a meal or even as a meal!

Melt the butter in a medium sauté pan over low heat. Add the garlic and salt and pepper, and cook until fragrant, about 4 minutes. Add your shrimp and cook for about 7 minutes. Make sure the shrimp are not completely cooked through. Add your pesto and let the shrimp finish cooking in the pesto sauce, about 4 minutes. Remove the pan from the heat and let the mixture cool before you add it to your salad or the lettuce and vegetables could wilt from the heat.

In a large serving bowl, toss your spring salad mix and romaine hearts. Add the cheeses, then sprinkle in your mushrooms, tomatoes, avocados, peppers, and the hard-boiled egg slices (if using). Add your pesto shrimp and mix well. Let sit for 30 minutes in a cooler or fridge. As you are serving this salad, add your balsamic dressing and mix well again so all the flavors come together.

Spinach Summer Salad

Serves 6

Salad

1 (10-ounce) bag spinach mix

1 cup halved red grapes

6 to 8 strawberries, hulled and sliced

½ cup chopped walnuts

Dressing

½ cup vegetable oil

¼ cup white wine vinegar

½ cup sugar

1 tablespoon horseradish sauce

2 tablespoons sesame seeds

2 tablespoons poppy seeds

This is a fresh and delicious salad that cools you off if you've had a long, hot day.

Toss all your salad ingredients together in a large bowl. In a medium bowl, combine the dressing ingredients and whisk well. Let the flavors come together 10 minutes, then give it another good whisking and pour it into the salad. Toss everything to mix well, then serve it immediately so the lettuce doesn't get oversaturated.

SAUCES

Parmesan Cheese Sauce

Makes 1 cup

4 tablespoons (½ stick) unsalted butter

2 tablespoons chopped garlic

Salt and black pepper

1 (1-pound) bar Parmesan cheese, crumbled

1 cup heavy whipping cream

¼ cup chicken broth

Melt the butter in a large sauté pan over medium heat. Add the garlic and salt and pepper, and cook until the garlic becomes fragrant. Add the Parmesan cheese, cream, broth, and more salt and pepper to your liking. Stir constantly and let it reduce and thicken. The sauce is done when you can dip a spoon in it and nothing drips off. If the sauce drips back into the sauté pan, you need to keep heating and stirring until it is creamy and ready to serve.

Pink Sauce

Makes 2 cups

1 (28-ounce) can crushed tomatoes

1 (15-ounce) can tomato sauce

Chopped garlic blend seasoning to your liking

Italian seasoning to your liking

Dried oregano to your liking

Salt and black pepper

3 tablespoons unsalted butter

3 tablespoons chopped garlic

2 tablespoons chopped shallot

½ cup heavy whipping cream

½ cup shredded Parmesan cheese

Dump the crushed tomatoes and tomato sauce in a medium saucepan. Season with the chopped garlic blend, Italian seasoning, oregano, and salt and pepper. Let simmer for about 15 minutes over low heat.

Melt your butter in a medium sauté pan over medium heat. Add your garlic, shallot, whipping cream, and some salt and pepper and let cook until the sauce starts to thicken, about 10 minutes. When you dip a spoon in it and there is just a little dripping, add the Parmesan cheese and let it melt until it's as thick as Alfredo sauce. Mix the tomato sauce and the cream sauce together to make a pink sauce.

This sauce is great with the Blue Cheese Meatballs on page 104.

NEVER TAKE A CAT CAMPING

One thing I have learned from being married to a schoolteacher is that it is like being married to a teenager. She is always right. So proving her wrong takes serious strategy with the wording of our discussions as well as considerable bravery. The day my wife announced she wanted to take the cat camping, my words were spoken delicately and well thought out: "Are you out of your freaking mind? NO!" That sentence had sounded completely different in my head.

My wife saw a single lady traveling in a Winnebago by herself with a cat and caught this wild notion that traveling with our kitty would be fun. The Winnebago cat lady would let her cat run free in camp to fulfill its constitutional kitty duty, leaving her RV cat box free. My wife visited with the lady and the cat for a few hours and soon had her mind made up that our cat should become a camper. The best part was watching my wife tell our two-year-old housecat, Dodger, about this new plan. She even bought a cat tent to "practice" on the back deck.

After she broke the news, the orange tabby gave her the typical cat look that said, "Feed me, scratch me, or otherwise don't speak to me unless spoken to!" Little did this cat know what was in store for him. We set out for McCall, Idaho, in the morning with a cat cage, litter box, water bowl, plastic bag full of cat food, a cat tent, and a bewildered cat who seemed to be thinking it was trade-in day and we were ditching him. Actually this thought had crossed my mind before, and Dodger knew it.

Once we set out on our adventure with Dodger in his cage, the meowing started and never really ended. We took him out and let him sit up front on my wife's lap like a spoiled cat. When he noticed our large windshield and the world passing by at sixty-five miles per hour, he had what is known as a "cat panic attack," also known as a "Catnictact." Okay, so I made that up. He started to hyperventilate and pant very heavily. My wife asked me what was happening and I once again tried to choose my words carefully. I told her that the cat was dying and it was her fault. This, too, had sounded very different in my head. The first thing that came to mind was to have the cat breathe into a paper sack with his head between his knees, but of course I didn't have a paper sack, so we put him back in the carrier and he calmed down, knowing he wasn't going to be in a head-on crash.

Shortly after we arrived at our camping spot my wife unfolded the "outdoor mesh cat condo tent." Don't ask where she found it, but she did. Within ten minutes a friendly camp fox was lurking around the corner, looking very happy to see that we had brought a delicious playmate. Of course the fox was laughing too hard to attack once he saw our cat step on a thorn and scream for help.

We moved the cat inside our "human-sized screen room" and put him on a long leash. Have you ever seen how a cat reacts to a full-sized body harness? They fall down like they just got shot and look at you with a questioning, "WHY?" Within three minutes of standing in his

full bondage harness, Dodger had stepped on a wasp, jumped six feet in the air, and started to run up the inside walls of the tent the same way motorcycles ride inside the globe of death. He eventually ran out of cat leash and hung himself over a lounge chair.

Once I regained my composure and untangled our distressed tabby, I put him inside our trailer with his litter box and got a blanket of apologies for my wife. We spent the rest of the day outside enjoying the 80°F temperature and a few beers before going back inside the trailer to an aromatic gift left in the litter box by one pissed-off cat.

So let's review: Our cat hyperventilated, stuck himself, got stung by a wasp, hung himself, and left a cat bomb that could have peeled paint off a wall. Now you know why you don't take a cat camping.

—Pat

Red Wine Mushroom Sauce

Makes ¾ cup

2 cups red wine

2 tablespoons olive oil

1 tablespoon chopped garlic

2 tablespoons finely chopped shallot

1 cup sliced white button mushrooms

1 cup sliced portabella mushrooms

Salt and black pepper

Pour the red wine in a medium sauté pan and bring to a simmer over low to medium heat. Let this reduce until the wine thickens up to a saucy texture, about 15 minutes, or until you dip a spoon in and nothing drips off.

Meanwhile, heat the olive oil in a medium sauté pan over medium heat. Add the garlic, shallot, and both types of mushrooms, and sauté until the mushrooms are cooked through, about 10 minutes.

Once the red wine has reduced (check by dipping a spoon in—if there are no drips, it's ready), add your mushrooms and let them cook over low heat for about 15 minutes, or until thickened. Season to taste with salt and pepper.

We recommend this red wine sauce over a nice piece of red meat, such as the Steak Milanese on page 92.

Amogio Sauce

Makes 1 cup

1 cup olive oil

8 tablespoons (1 stick) unsalted butter

½ cup lemon juice

1 tablespoon chopped garlic

1 tablespoon finely chopped shallot

1 tablespoon dried parsley

1 tablespoon dried basil

½ teaspoon crushed red pepper flakes

Salt and black pepper

Mix all the ingredients together in a medium saucepan over medium-high heat. Bring to a boil, then reduce the heat to low and simmer for 3 to 5 minutes.

Brown Sugar Sauce

Makes ¼ cup

4 tablespoons (½ stick) unsalted butter

3 tablespoons brown sugar

Melt your butter and sugar together in a small saucepan over low heat, stirring often, until fully combined.

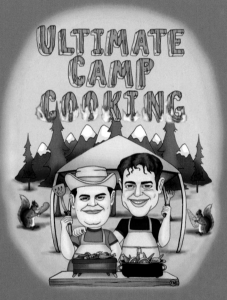

DESSERTS

Bread Pudding

Serves 8 to 10

1 tablespoon butter, softened

4 (6-inch) rolls, cubed and dried

2¾ cups raisins

7 large eggs

1 tablespoon ground nutmeg

1 tablespoon ground cinnamon

1 tablespoon vanilla extract

Pinch of salt

2 cups sugar

3 cups half-and-half

3 cups heavy whipping cream

Prepared caramel sauce, for serving

Preheat the oven to 325°F. Butter a 9 by 13 by 2-inch aluminum pan and toss your bread cubes in it.

In a large bowl, place your raisins, eggs, nutmeg, cinnamon, vanilla, salt, sugar, half-and-half, and cream, and mix well. Pour this over your bread cubes. Place the pan inside a larger pan and pour enough water into the larger pan to come about halfway up the sides of the bread pudding pan. This is called a hot water bath, and it lets the pudding steam and bake by indirect heat. Put it in the oven and bake for about 1 hour and 15 minutes, or until the biscuits pop up cooked through.

Take the pudding out of the water bath and set directly in the oven for 10 more minutes, or until it browns on top. Take it out of the oven and let it set for 30 minutes, then drizzle caramel sauce over it.

Monkey Bread

Serves 6 to 8

1 (16.3-ounce) can biscuits

2 tablespoons ground cinnamon

¼ cup granulated sugar

⅓ cup firmly packed brown sugar

3 tablespoons cold salted sweet cream butter, cut into ½-inch pieces

Cut each biscuit into quarters. Throw the pieces in a 1-gallon re-sealable plastic bag with the cinnamon and granulated sugar, seal it tightly, and shake until coated. Oil the insert of your Dutch oven and dump in the coated pieces. Sprinkle the brown sugar and butter chunks over the top.

Cover the Dutch oven, put 12 coals on top and 6 coals around the outside of the bottom (not underneath), and bake for about 30 minutes, or until the biscuits pop up cooked through. Remove the insert and flip it upside down into another pan. The butter and brown sugar will have sunk to the bottom and coated the bread so it looks like a Bundt cake. To serve it, just pull the pieces apart.

Bananas Foster

Serves 4 to 6

1½ cups maple syrup

3 ripe bananas cut evenly into ⅛-inch-thin slices

1 cup dark rum

½ cup chopped walnuts

Vanilla bean ice cream (we prefer Breyer's), for serving

In a large sauté pan, combine your maple syrup, bananas, and dark rum and cook on high heat until the alcohol burns off a bit, about 10 minutes. Lower the heat to medium, throw in your chopped walnuts, and cook until it thickens, about 5 minutes.

Scoop out a nice portion of vanilla ice cream into each serving bowl, pour the sauce over the ice cream, let it sit and melt a little, and then serve.

This is an easy, rich, and delicious recipe to impress anyone who joins you for a dinner party. You probably won't have any left, but if you do, it's more for you!

Dutch Apple Biscuits

Serves 6 to 8

1 (16.3-ounce) can biscuits

2 tablespoons granulated sugar

2 tablespoons ground cinnamon

1 (14-ounce) can sweetened condensed milk

1 (21-ounce) can apple pie filling

⅓ cup firmly packed brown sugar

3 tablespoons cold salted sweet cream butter, cut into ½-inch pieces

2 teaspoons vanilla extract

Rip the biscuits into small pieces, roll them into balls, and place them in a 1-gallon resealable plastic bag. Add the granulated sugar and cinnamon, seal the bag tightly, and shake well. Dump the biscuits balls into your greased Dutch oven insert and make sure all the biscuit balls are covered with sugar and cinnamon. Pour the sweetened condensed milk and apple pie filling over the top, then add the brown sugar, butter pieces, and vanilla extract. Mix well.

Place the insert in your Dutch oven, cover it, and put 12 coals on top and 6 coals around the outside of the bottom (not underneath). Cook for 1 hour and 20 minutes, or until the biscuits are cooked through, checking occasionally to make sure they are cooking evenly and not burning. If so, pull out, mix well, and place back in, taking off some coals.

Strawberry Dump Cake

Serves 6 to 8

1 (10-ounce) can strawberry pie filling

1 (18.25-ounce) package chocolate cake mix

1 (3-ounce) chocolate bar (we prefer Hershey's)

2 tablespoons heavy whipping cream

1 (8-ounce) container nondairy whipped topping (we prefer Cool Whip)

¼ cup coffee liqueur (we prefer Kahlúa)

Take your Dutch oven insert and dump in the strawberry pie filling, the cake mix, and the broken-up chocolate bar. Add the cream and mix briefly. Put the insert in the Dutch oven, cover it, and put about 8 coals around the top edge and 4 coals around the outside of the bottom (not underneath). Cook for 25 to 30 minutes, or until the chocolate has completely melted. You may want to stir it after about 20 minutes of cooking, but it's not mandatory. Some of the batter may stick together if you do not stir thoroughly.

Once the ingredients are fully cooked, scoop out a nice amount into some serving bowls, lay some whipped topping on each one, and drizzle coffee liqueur across the top.

You will have several more friends after they taste this delight. Mike ate so much one time he got drunk and passed out with chocolate all over his face. It looked like he made out with an engine!

Soggy Weekend

When I was thirteen years old, I got into backpacking with my best friend, Jeff; we were the youngest mountaineers in our minds, and ready for adventure.

Jeff's parents told us they were headed to a favorite camp spot in Stanley, Idaho, in their trailer. Of course being mountaineering experts, camping in a trailer was not for us. So we had them drop us off on the way up to the Sawtooth Mountain Range at the bottom of Bear Creek so we could spend the weekend backpacking alone in the wilderness while they stayed in a stuffy trailer.

It was Friday morning at 10:00 A.M. one day in May when Jeff's parents dropped us off at Bear Creek and told us they would be back Sunday afternoon around 1:00 P.M. As the truck drove off, Jeff and I looked around the deserted parking lot. Just on the other side was an empty campground. We were all alone, wondering if other backpackers would be coming.

Our plan was to hike three miles back to a lake and spend the weekend seeking adventure in the mountain range near a small river called Bear Creek. It never occurred to me why they called it Bear Creek until his parents left. Oh, well. Though his parents were only ten miles away, to us it felt like there wasn't another human for more like 300 miles.

We had strapped the packs on our backs, double-checked the map, and started for the trail when raindrops started to fall. We stood under a tree for a while, waiting for it to slow down, but it never did. We decided to set up camp in the vacant campground!

It started to get dark and the rain continued as we huddled in our "three-man tent" that actually seemed built for one, and we decided to leave first thing in the morning. We cooked dinner outside the door of the tent while it poured rain around us. The cold chill started setting in and we could see our own breath. We were prepared, though, as we were young adventure-seeking mountaineers.

After a long night being kept up by the thunder, wind, rain and the thought of the name Bear Creek, it finally became light outside. The only problem was there was no sun, just rain . . . rain . . . and more rain. We stuck our heads out of our tent to cook breakfast, using the overhang to keep the eggs from getting wet. We also came to the realization that nobody was going to camp next to us that weekend.

By noon, we had decided not to make the hike to the top of the mountain, seeing instead that building an ark was in order. Then we wondered what time his parents would show up to save us from the monsoon. Having no cell phones back then or dry wood for a signal fire, we tried telepathic communication. Imagine two thirteen-year-olds with their hands on their heads, concentrating.

The rain continued into the evening, never letting up, and there was no sight of his parents. Water started to seep into the floor of the tent, creating two pissed-off teenagers. We played cards, talked about girls, and cursed his parents for their abandonment. We ate all our snacks out of boredom and cooked our last dinner under the soaked nylon porch.

Our minds were fried from solitary confinement because the only time we left the tent was to relieve ourselves. Our backs hurt, our feet were cold, and our clothes were wet. But at least I was smart enough to sneak in some vodka to mix with our Tang. Wait, I was thirteen. Never mind that part. That didn't help the bathroom breaks.

Sunday morning finally arrived and still no sun, even though the rain slowed from a downpour to a steady drizzle. It was still too early to believe our rescue would take place. We figured if they didn't come Saturday, then noon Sunday it was.

Jeff's parents rolled in right on schedule with big smiles on their faces and giggles under their breath. Two soggy, angry teens stood in ankle-deep water in the parking lot. I realized that his parents were teaching us a lesson: Old people suck (and trailers are very cool to have when it rains for three days straight).

—Pat

Blueberry Dumplings

Serves 5 to 7

1 cup all-purpose flour

1½ cups granulated sugar

1 tablespoon baking powder

½ cup unsalted butter, at room temperature

½ cup 2% milk

Pinch of salt

1 (21-ounce) can blueberry pie filling

1½ quarts vanilla bean ice cream, for serving (we prefer Breyer's)

Combine the flour, 1 cup of sugar, the baking powder, butter, milk, and salt in a medium bowl, and mix well to form a dough.

In a large pan over low heat, combine the remaining ½ cup of sugar, the blueberry pie filling, and 1 cup water, and bring to a simmer.

Pinch off a small dough ball (about 3 tablespoons), roll into little balls, and place into the simmering blueberry mixture. Let the dumplings cook in the sauce until they have cooked through, about 7 minutes.

Spoon the dumplings and blueberry sauce into serving bowls and scoop some vanilla ice cream over it. Make sure to take it slow and not bite your tongue off, as this is a hard recipe to not completely devour!

Blueberry Cobbler

Serves 4 to 6

½ cup all-purpose flour

½ cup granulated sugar

½ tablespoon baking powder

1 cup heavy whipping cream

3 tablespoons unsalted butter, at room temperature

1 cup fresh blueberries

Confectioners' sugar, for sprinkling on top

In a large bowl, combine the flour, granulated sugar, baking powder, cream, and butter, and mix until it makes a sticky dough.

Grease 6 individual ramekins so there is no sticking after cooking. Drop about 4 tablespoons (¼ cup) of dough into each ramekin and use your fingers to spread it evenly across the bottoms and up the sides to form a cup for the filling. Put a few spoonfuls of blueberries in each cup.

Put the ramekins in your Dutch oven and pour a little hot water in the bottom of the Dutch oven to the middle of the ramekin. Cover the Dutch oven and put 8 coals on top and 4 coals around the outside of the bottom (not underneath). Cook for 35 to 40 minutes, or until the dough has cooked through. Sprinkle some confectioners' sugar on top before serving.

This awesome dessert blows people away because of how gourmet it is and how easy it is to make in the outdoors!

Camp S'more Pies

Serves 4 to 6

4 to 6 tiny premade graham cracker pie crusts

1 candy bar of each (Snickers, Butterfinger, Baby Ruth, and Reese's Peanut Butter Cups work well), broken up, for topping

1 (10-ounce) bag marshmallows (small or large)

Nondairy whipped topping (we prefer Cool Whip) or vanilla bean ice cream (we prefer Breyer's), for serving

Fill each mini pie crust with broken-up pieces of candy bars. You can mix up the candy bar pieces and put several different varieties in each pie. Cover the candy bar pieces with the marshmallows. You may need to tear up the large marshmallows into smaller pieces.

Lay the pies in your Dutch oven, cover it, and put 6 coals on top and 4 coals around the outside of the bottom (not underneath). Cook for about 10 minutes, or until the marshmallows brown on top. Watch these closely, as they will cook fast and you don't want to burn them. Once the s'mores pies are done, cover them with whipped topping or vanilla ice cream and serve.

Acknowledgments

I want to thank all the people out there who stink at cooking. It was my parents' inability to cook that gave me the inspiration to give it a shot. How bad could I be in comparison to my family? My first cooking job was in the summer of '95 at a greasy spoon named the Brewster Coffee Shop in Cape Cod, Massachusetts. It was a small truck stop café that served the early risers with mediocre coffee and edible omelets. I was pushed into the position as prep cook. The manager, an exhausted, lonely, rundown woman who chain-smoked, thought I was cute and wanted me to take over the former grill cook's position, as he was strung out on pills and alcohol. It was all brand new to me, as I didn't even know how to hold a spatula correctly. But I was a smart kid and a real quick learner, so I picked it up quickly and fell in love with the fast-paced, organized aspect of preparing a dish. You need precise timing to make a meal come together. Everything needs to be perfect, and all the food needs to finish perfectly at the same time, ready to be served. I loved staying overwhelmingly busy too as it seemed like time passed faster that way. I actually took pride in making artistic plates that people were proud to dig into. Seeing people eat your food, smiling and going about their day, became a new passion for me. There was a sense of pride I never experienced before. It got to the point where I was laughing, joking, and working all at the same time, which I didn't think existed at a job. I learned that the real personalities of most restaurants are in the kitchen. I also quickly learned that women love a man who can cook! (Not that I needed help in that category!) There's something erotic and sensual about food. I think it's everyone's passion whether you like to eat or not. Food is sexy and everyone wants a piece of it. I fell in love with cooking almost immediately, like a summer crush that wouldn't go away.

As the summer of '95 crept to an end, one of my finest summers to date, I was saddened by the notion that I may not be

cooking anymore. I really loved my job, the creativeness and unpredictability of the kitchen. I thought to myself, maybe I could find a nice restaurant at college. I could work part time and still have that rush of being on the line. That's exactly what happened: The day I arrived at school I applied at the busiest and coolest restaurant in town and got the job. I didn't look back from there and I've been in a kitchen ever since. You have to love the craft, and if you are not completely engulfed by it you will be weeded out quickly by the pace and stress, but if you love it the way it needs to be loved, you will not work another day in your life.

Mike Faverman

I would like to thank Mike Faverman for helping me realize my dream of camp cooking and taking care of the business aspect of our company. Thanks to all of those at the Affinity Group, especially Tom and Lorisa for their constant care of detail and helping us grow. I want to thank my fellow camp mates, Sandy and Dexter, Doug and Kelly, Albert and Colonel Michelle Woods for many nights around the campfire exchanging recipes and stories and sharing good food. Colonel Woods, thank you for the green bean recipe; you have the mouth of an oil rig waitress and we love you for that!

I also want to thank my longtime friend from high school, Ted, for lending me a couple of recipes from the kitchen and changing the name of many of my original recipes to Ted's Chili, Ted's Wings, Ted's Sugar Bacon, and Ted's Pasta.

Finally, I would like to thank my wife, Karen, for giving me the freedom to cook for the entire camp and work on my recipes, and for putting up with my many weeks of travel throughout the year. You have always believed in me even when my dreams reach the moon.

Pat Mac

Metric Conversions and Equivalents

Metric Conversion Formulas

TO CONVERT	MULTIPLY
Ounces to grams	Ounces by 28.35
Pounds to kilograms	Pounds by 0.454
Teaspoons to milliliters	Teaspoons by 4.93
Tablespoons to milliliters	Tablespoons by 14.79
Fluid ounces to milliliters	Fluid ounces by 29.57
Cups to milliliters	Cups by 236.59
Cups to liters	Cups by 0.236
Pints to liters	Pints by 0.473
Quarts to liters	Quarts by 0.946
Gallons to liters	Gallons by 3.785
Inches to centimeters	Inches by 2.54

Approximate Metric Equivalents
VOLUME

¼ teaspoon	1 milliliter
½ teaspoon	2.5 milliliters
¾ teaspoon	4 milliliters
1 teaspoon	5 milliliters
1¼ teaspoons	6 milliliters
1½ teaspoons	7.5 milliliters
1¾ teaspoons	8.5 milliliters
2 teaspoons	10 milliliters
1 tablespoon (½ fluid ounce)	15 milliliters
2 tablespoons (1 fluid ounce)	30 milliliters
¼ cup	60 milliliters
⅓ cup	80 milliliters
½ cup (4 fluid ounces)	120 milliliters
⅔ cup	160 milliliters
¾ cup	180 milliliters
1 cup (8 fluid ounces)	240 milliliters
1¼ cups	300 milliliters
1½ cups (12 fluid ounces)	360 milliliters
1⅔ cups	400 milliliters
2 cups (1 pint)	460 milliliters
3 cups	700 milliliters
4 cups (1 quart)	0.95 liter
1 quart plus ¼ cup	1 liter
4 quarts (1 gallon)	3.8 liters

WEIGHT

¼ ounce	7 grams
½ ounce	14 grams
¾ ounce	21 grams
1 ounce	28 grams
1¼ ounces	35 grams
1½ ounces	42.5 grams
1⅔ ounces	45 grams
2 ounces	57 grams
3 ounces	85 grams
4 ounces (¼ pound)	113 grams
5 ounces	142 grams
6 ounces	170 grams
7 ounces	198 grams
8 ounces (½ pound)	227 grams
16 ounces (1 pound)	454 grams
35.25 ounces (2.2 pounds)	1 kilogram

LENGTH

⅛ inch	3 millimeters
¼ inch	6 millimeters
½ inch	1¼ centimeters
1 inch	2½ centimeters
2 inches	5 centimeters
2½ inches	6 centimeters
4 inches	10 centimeters
5 inches	13 centimeters
6 inches	15¼ centimeters
12 inches (1 foot)	30 centimeters

Common Ingredients and Their Approximate Equivalents

1 cup uncooked rice = 225 grams

1 cup all-purpose flour = 140 grams

1 stick butter (4 ounces • ½ cup • 8 tablespoons) = 110 grams

1 cup butter (8 ounces • 2 sticks • 16 tablespoons) = 220 grams

1 cup brown sugar, firmly packed = 225 grams

1 cup granulated sugar = 200 grams

Oven Temperatures

To convert Fahrenheit to Celsius, subtract 32 from Fahrenheit, multiply the result by 5, then divide by 9.

DESCRIPTION	FAHRENHEIT	CELSIUS	BRITISH GASMARK
Very cool	200°	95°	0
Very cool	225°	110°	¼
Very cool	250°	120°	½
Cool	275°	135°	1
Cool	300°	150°	2
Warm	325°	165°	3
Moderate	350°	175°	4
Moderately hot	375°	190°	5
Fairly hot	400°	200°	6
Hot	425°	220°	7
Very hot	450°	230°	8
Very hot	475°	245°	9

Information compiled from a variety of sources, including *Recipes into Type* by Joan Whitman and Dolores Simon (Newton, MA: Biscuit Books, 2000); *The New Food Lover's Companion* by Sharon Tyler Herbst (Hauppauge, NY: Barron's, 1995); and *Rosemary Brown's Big Kitchen Instruction Book* (Kansas City, MO: Andrews McMeel, 1998).

Photo Credits

Food photographs and photographs of Mike Faverman and Pat Mac on the following pages copyright © 2011 by Mike Faverman and Pat Mac: 1, 3, 4, 8, 10, 14, 16, 19, 27, 28, 32, 37, 38, 44, 46, 52, 60, 62, 63, 73, 74, 76, 77, 78, 83, 90, 92, 95, 103, 106, 109, 116, 118, 120, 125, 132, 134, 135, 140, 144, 149, 164, 166, 170, 174, 175, 184

Food photographs and photographs of Mike Faverman and Pat Mac on the following pages copyright © 2011 by Marc Kallweit: iii, iv, v, vi–vii, 2, 24, 30, 33, 40, 41, 42, 50, 57, 59, 68, 69, 70, 72, 81, 87, 89, 105, 111, 114, 115, 127, 136, 139, 141, 142, 147, 154, 160, 161, 162–163, 167, 168, 171, 182–183, 185, 187, 193

pp. ii, viii, 2–7, 9, 10–16, 18–29, 34, 39–41, 45–46, 49, 51, 52–55, 58, 64–67, 71, 74–75, 78–80, 82, 84–85, 90–91, 96, 98–102, 108–109, 112–113, 121, 124–125, 128–131, 137–138, 142–143, 150–151, 154–155, 157–160, 165–166, 171–172, 176–178, 188–190, 194–195 © Candi4636 | Dreamstime.com

p. iii © Cflorinc | Dreamstime.com

p. v, top © Davidebner | Dreamstime.com

p. v, bottom © Darren Baker | Dreamstime.com

p. vi, center left © Monkey Business Images | Dreamstime.com

p. vi, center right © Susy56 | Dreamstime.com

p. vi, bottom © Fred Stillings | Dreamstime.com

p. vii © Ryan Pike | Dreamstime.com

p. 5 © Dennis Cox | Dreamstime.com

pp. 9, 21 © Melissa Carroll

p. 12 © 4kodiak | Dreamstime.com

pp. 22–23, 29, 45–46, 54–55, 58, 64–65, 71, 82, 98–102, 112–113, 121, 128–131, 137–138, 150–151, 157–158, 165–166, 176–178, 188–190. By permission. From Merriam-Webster's Learner's Dictionary © 2010 by Merriam-Webster, Incorporated (www.LearnersDictionary.com).

pp. 23, 65 © Denis Tabler | Dreamstime.com

p. 24 © Tom Lewis

pp. 31, 133 © Andy Burnfield (wood background)

p. 34 © Liz Van Steenburgh | Dreamstime.com

p. 35 © photovideostock

p. 43 © Rosemary Buffoni | Dreamstime.com

p. 54 © Viktor Kitaykin

p. 71 © Penywise | Dreamstime.com

p. 90 © Tyler Olson | Dreamstime.com

p. 93 © Goce Risteski | Dreamstime.com

p. 100 © Michael Wright

p. 109 © Beth Van Trees | Dreamstime.com

p. 112 © Eric Isselée

p. 121 © Anna Sevkovich

p. 137 © Goce Risteski | Dreamstime.com

p. 153 © Clayton Hansen

p. 157 © Ene | Dreamstime.com

p. 173 © Wojtek Kryczka

p. 177 © David Thompson | Dreamstime.com

p. 181 © Johann Helgason | Dreamstime.com

p. 189 © Richard Nelson | Dreamstime.com

Index